Excel

Get the Results You Want

Years 3–4 Opportunity Class Reading Tests

Donna Gibbs

PASCAL PRESS

Completely new edition incorporating 2021 Opportunity Class test changes

Reprinted 2024 (twice)

ISBN 978 1 74125 706 9

Pascal Press Pty Ltd
PO Box 250
Glebe NSW 2037
(02) 9198 1748
www.pascalpress.com.au

Publisher: Vivienne Joannou
Project editor: Mark Dixon
Edited by Mark Dixon
Answers checked by Dale Little
Cover by DiZign Pty Ltd
Typeset by Grizzly Graphics (Leanne Richters)
Printed by Vivar Printing/Green Giant Press

Contents

ABOUT THE OPPORTUNITY CLASS TEST

The NSW Opportunity Class Placement Test is required for placement in an Opportunity Class in a NSW public school. This type of class offers an extra challenge for academically gifted students with high potential in Years 5 and 6. Selection is based on academic merit.

Students are usually in Year 4 when they apply for opportunity class placement and take the test.

Details are available at: https://education.nsw.gov.au.

The tests were updated in 2021 with a greater emphasis on literacy, thinking skills, mathematical reasoning and problem solving. The General Ability Test has been replaced by a Thinking Skills Test. The new NSW Opportunity Class Placement Test adjusts and balances the weighting given to the Reading, Thinking Skills and Mathematical Reasoning components; these are now equal. These changes were in response to the findings of the 2018 Rrview of Selective Education Access report, commissioned by the NSW Department of Education.

The NSW Opportunity Class Placement Test consists of three multiple-choice sections:

- **Reading** (25 questions in 30 minutes)
- **Mathematical Reasoning** (35 questions in 40 minutes)
- **Thinking Skills** (30 questions in 30 minutes).

Reading test

The question format for the Reading test varies from subsection to subsection. At the time of writing, the question format is as follows for the four subsections:

Literary prose text—multiple-choice questions on a single text or extract from a text

Poetry—multiple-choice questions about a poem or extract from a poem

Factual text—a task which asks you to place sentences or phrases into an information text in a sequence that makes sense (a cloze task)

Varied short texts—matching descriptive statements to four short texts on the same theme but with different content and written in different styles or from different perspectives.

Each question in the NSW Opportunity Class Placement Test is multiple choice. This means you have to choose the correct answer from the given options.

Mini tests

This section gives you examples of the types of questions and texts likely to be included in the NSW Opportunity Class Reading test. This is followed by an explanation of strategies that can be used to help improve the use of these skills.

As an introduction to the process of choosing the correct answer for the different types of questions asked, some shorter sample texts with fewer questions are provided in this section. There are four mini tests (literary prose text, poetry, factual text and varied short texts) to match the four different sections of the test. These are accompanied by suggested strategies for finding the correct answer for each question. In this way students will learn more about the processes involved in completing the test. Once this section has been carefully worked through, you will be ready to attempt the sample tests.

Sample tests

This section consists of ten sample tests based on the actual Reading test. Each test has been carefully constructed to reflect the length, format and level of the actual tests.

Learning to manage the time available for completing a Reading test is an important skill to develop. It is unwise to spend a lot of time on a question that puzzles you because it may mean you won't have time to finish the test. However, once you have completed the test it would be very useful to spend time thinking more about such questions and their answers. This will help you prepare for similar questions in the future.

The following suggested procedure for working through the book can be adapted to individual needs related to your level of ability and learning style.

- Work through the mini tests until you feel confident you have grasped how to attempt the sample tests.
- Complete the first sample test.
- Keep a record of the time you take and your score.
- Read through the answers carefully, noting the reasons given for both correct and incorrect answers. This is a very important part of the process as it helps deepen your understanding of the subject.
- When you understand all the questions and answers you have completed, move on to the next sample test.
- Keep alert to the patterns that emerge in your test results, as this can reveal areas of weakness that need further practice.

Skills and strategies

The skills of analysing, identifying, interpreting, comparing, predicting and evaluating will help provide answers to the different types of test questions in reading comprehension, an important and complex segment of the NSW Opportunity Class Placement Test.

To answer reading-comprehension questions you will draw on skills such as:

- analysing the purpose of a text

- analysing the topic of a text
- analysing the effects of specific language choices
- analysing point(s) of view within a text
- identifying mood, atmosphere or tone
- identifying the meaning of words and phrases in context
- identifying how information and ideas are related
- identifying how information and ideas are organised or sequenced
- interpreting meanings by connecting aspects of a text with your existing knowledge
- interpreting meanings by working out what is implied
- comparing aspects of a text such as forms, structures, ideas and language use
- comparing whole texts in a variety of ways
- predicting or forecasting what could occur by using evidence from a text
- making judgements about a writer's values and attitudes
- making judgements about characters and their relationships with others
- evaluating the effectiveness of a text.

The different types of questions will include:

- finding facts in the text
- inferring meaning by reading between the lines
- weighing up evidence from the text to make judgements.

The test questions will be asked about a range of texts or of extracts from the texts. These could include:

- short stories, novels, poetry or drama
- informative or persuasive articles
- diaries, autobiographies or biographies
- speeches, debates, letters, reviews, conversations or recounts

- reports, observations, descriptions or instructions
- brochures, charts, diagrams or maps.

The strategies listed below detail ways to become better at understanding and appreciating what you read. They should become a normal part of your daily life.

- Read widely (absolutely the most important).
- Think critically about the text both as you read and when you have finished reading. What is the writer trying to say? How does the material make you feel? Is it funny? Is it sad? Does it make you think? Can you identify with it? Is it effective?
- Talk about what you read with others. Compare opinions and share ideas.
- If you are unsure of a word meaning, try to work it out from its context and from your knowledge of how words are formed. Use clues provided by prefixes, suffixes or words with similar origins. Have a dictionary on hand to confirm or extend your understanding.
- Always ask for help if you are puzzled by anything in your reading matter.

Below are some specific strategies to use when answering reading-comprehension questions.

1 Skim the text to gather a general idea of what kind of text it is, then read through the questions quickly (not the possible answers at this stage). This will alert you to key aspects of the text and give you an overview of what will be asked.

2 Read the text through carefully. If there is time and you are a fast reader, read it twice.

3 Take careful note of the title if there is one. It can be a strong lead as to the purpose, line of thinking and tone of the material.

4 Look out for clues as to the purpose of the text as you read. Is it telling a story, persuading you to do something, explaining ways to solve a problem, creating a mood or presenting different viewpoints about a topic? This understanding will inform the way you answer the questions.

5 Take note of the topic sentences (usually the first sentence) in each paragraph as you read. These sentences give an indication of what the rest of the paragraph is about and help you when referring back to answer questions.

6 When answering the questions:
- read all the possible answers before deciding on the best one (and on the way cross out any that are obviously wrong)
- look back at the text to check your answer
- look for clues in the surrounding context.

7 Use your time wisely. Multiple-choice questions are usually of equal mark value so it is unwise to spend too much time on one question. Leave any puzzling questions with your best guess answer and go back to it if you have time at the end.

8 When you check your answers, don't rush the process of seeing why an answer is right or wrong. There is a lot of information included in the answers that can help you improve your grasp of the concepts involved in reading and writing. This is a valuable way to build the depth of your knowledge and understanding.

Advice to students

Each question in the NSW Opportunity Class Placement Test is multiple choice. This means you have to choose the correct answer from the given options.

We have included sample answer sheets in this book for you to practise on. Note that from 2025, however, the NSW Opportunity Class Placement Test will change to a computer-based test.

Reading answer sheet

Mark your answers here.

To answer each question, fill in the appropriate circle for your chosen answer.

Use a pencil. If you make a mistake or change your mind, erase and try again.

You can make extra copies of this answer sheet to mark your answers to all the Sample Reading tests in this book.

1 A B C D
   ○ ○ ○ ○

2 A B C D
   ○ ○ ○ ○

3 A B C D
   ○ ○ ○ ○

4 A B C D
   ○ ○ ○ ○

5 A B C D
   ○ ○ ○ ○

6 A B C D
   ○ ○ ○ ○

7 A B C D
   ○ ○ ○ ○

8 A B C D
   ○ ○ ○ ○

9 A B C D
   ○ ○ ○ ○

10 A B C D
    ○ ○ ○ ○

11 A B C D
    ○ ○ ○ ○

12 A B C D E F G
    ○ ○ ○ ○ ○ ○ ○

13 A B C D E F G
    ○ ○ ○   ○ ○ ○
          ○

14 A B C D E F G
    ○ ○ ○ ○ ○ ○ ○

15 A B C D E F G
    ○ ○ ○ ○ ○ ○ ○

16 A B C D E F G
    ○ ○ ○ ○ ○ ○ ○

17 A B C D E F G
    ○ ○ ○ ○ ○ ○ ○

18 A B C D
    ○ ○ ○ ○

19 A B C D
    ○ ○ ○ ○

20 A B C D
    ○ ○ ○ ○

21 A B C D
    ○ ○ ○ ○

22 A B C D
    ○ ○ ○ ○

23 A B C D
    ○ ○ ○ ○

24 A B C D
    ○ ○ ○ ○

25 A B C D
    ○ ○ ○ ○

MINI TEST 1

10 MIN

Read the text below then answer the questions.

The Wind in the Willows

They reached the carriage-drive of Toad Hall to find, as Badger had anticipated, a shiny new motor-car, of great size, painted a bright red (Toad's favourite colour), standing in front of the house. As they neared the door it was flung open, and Mr. Toad, arrayed in goggles, cap, gaiters, and enormous overcoat, came swaggering down the steps, drawing on his gauntleted gloves.

'Hullo! come on, you fellows!' he cried cheerfully on catching sight of them. 'You're just in time to come with me for a jolly – to come for a jolly – for a – er –jolly –'

His hearty accents faltered and fell away as he noticed the stern unbending look on the countenances of his silent friends, and his invitation remained unfinished.

[...]

'You knew it must come to this, sooner or later, Toad,' the Badger explained severely. 'You've disregarded all the warnings we've given you, you've gone on squandering the money your father left you, and you're getting us animals a bad name in the district by your furious driving and your smashes and your rows with the police. Independence is all very well, but we animals never allow our friends to make fools of themselves beyond a certain limit; and that limit you've reached. Now, you're a good fellow in many respects, and I don't want to be too hard on you. I'll make one more effort to bring you to reason. You will come with me into the smoking-room, and there you will hear some facts about yourself; and we'll see whether you come out of that room the same Toad that you went in.'

He took Toad firmly by the arm, led him into the smoking-room, and closed the door behind them.

'*That's* no good!' said the Rat contemptuously. '*Talking* to Toad'll never cure him. He'll *say* anything.'

From *The Wind in the Willows* by Kenneth Grahame

Interpreting meanings by working out what is implied

1 Toad doesn't finish his invitation mainly because
   A he is shy.
   B he senses his friends don't like his car.
   C he realises his friends are seriously annoyed with him.
   D he notices his friends' silence.

ACTIVITY: You need to look for meanings that aren't directly stated in the text. These meanings will be suggested or hinted at by clues that alert you to what is implied.

STRATEGY: You need to think about the sequence of events to work out the reason Toad fails to finish his invitation. (Note: If a question includes a word such as 'mainly', it implies there could be two or more answers that are correct and the most correct needs to be chosen.)

Badger and Rat arrive to see Toad's shiny new red car and then Toad himself staggering down the steps, dressed in all his driving gear, ready to take off on one of his jaunts. You can work out their alarm about Toad's bad behaviour will be confirmed. At first Toad remains oblivious to their mood and cheerfully invites his friends to join him on his drive. He is so absorbed in his own pleasures that it takes him a while to notice their silence and the stern expressions on their faces. It is when it finally dawns on him that Badger and Rat are looking disapprovingly at him, rather than admiringly as he'd imagined, that he begins to stumble over his words and his invitation peters out.

Now look at options **A–D** and decide which best answers the question.

Making judgements about a character

2 Badger's treatment of Toad can be described as
   A unjustified.
   B cowardly.
   C cruel.
   D fair-minded.

ACTIVITY: You need to consider all the information you are given about the character—their words and actions, their relationships, and what others think or feel about them. You need to think critically to make a judgement.

STRATEGY: You need to make a judgement based on evidence about what the character says and does in the text in relation to your own knowledge and understanding.

Badger sees himself as a kind of moral leader of the animals whose duty it is to make Toad see the error of his ways. When Badger tells Toad of the animals' concern, he speaks severely and doesn't hold back from mentioning Toad's crimes. At the same time he confirms he and Rat are his friends and that they know he has his good points. He says he is prepared to make one more effort to bring Toad to his senses and chooses to do this in a room where they'll be alone. This is presumably to keep his criticism of Toad's character private rather than as a matter of further public shame.

Now look at options **A–D** and decide which best answers the question.

Identifying the meaning of words or phrases in context

3 The word 'contemptuously' tells us Rat feels _____ Badger's planning to talk further with Toad.

   A admiring of

   B scornful of

   C pleased about

   D annoyed by

ACTIVITY: You need to critically consider the meaning of the word or phrase in relation to the thoughts and ideas connected to it in context. (The context is everything that influences, acts upon or is connected with the language choices within a text.)

STRATEGY: You need to work out what meaning the word has from the way it is said as well as the situation in which it is used. You can also think about any clues the word provides from your knowledge of how words are formed.

Rat speaks 'contemptuously' immediately after he realises Badger is going to try to cure Toad by talking to him. The italics used for the words Rat uses—'*That's*', '*Talking*', '*say*'—emphasise how strongly Rat feels that talking won't cure Toad of his crimes. In other words he is critical of the idea and the italics emphasise that he feels this criticism very strongly!

Now look at options **A–D** and decide which best answers the question.

Read the poem by Mary Howett below then answer the questions.

The Spider and the Fly

'Will you walk into my parlour?' said the Spider to the Fly,
'' Tis the prettiest little parlour that ever you did spy;
The way into my parlour is up a winding stair,
And I have many curious things to shew when you are there.'
'Oh no, no,' said the little Fly, 'to ask me is in vain,
For who goes up your winding stair can ne'er come down again.'

[...]

The Spider turned him round about, and went into his den,
For well he knew the silly Fly would soon come back again:
So he wove a subtle web, in a little corner sly,
And set his table ready, to dine upon the Fly.
Then he came out to his door again, and merrily did sing,
'Come hither, hither, pretty Fly, with the pearl and silver wing;
Your robes are green and purple – there's a crest upon your head;
Your eyes are like the diamond bright, but mine are dull as lead!'

Alas, alas! how very soon this silly little Fly,
Hearing his wily, flattering words, came slowly flitting by;
With buzzing wings she hung aloft, then near and nearer drew,
Thinking only of her brilliant eyes, and green and purple hue –
Thinking only of her crested head – poor foolish thing! At last,
Up jumped the cunning Spider, and fiercely held her fast.
He dragged her up his winding stair, into his dismal den,
Within his little parlour – but she ne'er came out again!

And now dear little children, who may this story read,
To idle, silly flattering words, I pray you ne'er give heed:
Unto an evil counsellor, close heart and ear and eye,
And take a lesson from this tale, of the Spider and the Fly.

Analysing the point of view within a text

1 The story is narrated by

    A the Spider.

    B the Fly.

    C an evil counsellor.

    D the poet.

ACTIVITY: You need to work out from whose perspective the poem is told. The narrator, who is the teller of the story, sometimes understands more about the characters and their motivations than they are aware of themselves.

STRATEGY: Think about all the voices you can hear in the poem. Both the Spider and the Fly speak. However, another voice describes their interaction and what happens to them.

Now look at options **A–D** and decide which best answers the question.

Making judgements about a writer's values and attitudes

2 Which saying most closely represents the moral of the poem?

    A Don't put all your eggs in one basket.

    B Don't listen to flattery as it can be dangerous.

    C Don't count your chickens before they're hatched.

    D Imitation is the sincerest form of flattery.

ACTIVITY: You need to work out the writer's attitude to the characters and events in the poem so you can identify the moral that can be drawn from the story. Sometimes this is implied; at other times it is directly stated. (Fables which are often about animal characters usually state the moral clearly.)

STRATEGY: You can work out this poem is like a fable due to the presence of animal characters. The story told about the activities of the Spider and the Fly builds towards a moral that can be drawn from what happens.

Now look at options **A–D** and decide which best answers the question.

Read the text below then answer the questions.

Four sentences have been removed from the text. Choose from the sentences (**A–D**) the one which fits each gap (**1–3**). There is one extra sentence which you do not need to use.

Evonne Goolagong

The Goolagong family is descended from the Wiradgeri people. During the 1950s, when Evonne was growing up, Federal and State laws tended to treat First Australians differently from the non-Indigenous. **1** _____ For First Nations children to be unwelcome at places such as tennis clubs and swimming pools was not at all unusual.

Evonne had a passion for ball games from a very young age. **2** _____ Her dad even made her a wooden tennis racquet for her to play with and she practised with that. Although she wasn't allowed to play at her local court, she watched over the fence and listened and learned from the coaches. Eventually, the manager of her local tennis club rewarded her persistence and allowed her on to the court.

Her reputation spread and a Sydney tennis coach, Vic Edwards, invited her to move to Sydney. Soon Evonne began to win championships and build a stunning career. In 1971 and 1976, she was ranked the number one player in the world.

Her home town, Barellan, turned 100 years old in 2009. **3** _____ It is an exact 20:1 scale replica of her famous Dunlop wooden racquet measuring 13.8 metres long. It is placed in the Evonne Goolagong Park in her honour.

A	The story goes that a lucky find of a tennis ball under the wheel of her father's car kept her happily occupied for long stretches of time.
B	Part of their celebrations involved the building of 'The Big Tennis Racquet'.
C	It was not until 1961 that all First Australians were given the right to vote, for example.
D	The name of the town comes from a Wiradgeri word meaning the meeting of the waters.

Identifying how information and ideas are sequenced

ACTIVITY: You need to recognise that sequencing involves putting ideas and information in a logical order. In order to work out how ideas are connected to each other within a text, you need to consider what goes before and after, and how this fits into the whole.

STRATEGY: Read the entire passage first so you know what it is about. Then read the missing sentences. Find the space numbered 1 and think about the subject of the paragraph in which it occurs. Look closely at the sentence before and after the space and work out the sequence of ideas and information. Now select the sentence from A–D that best fills the space where a sentence has been removed. Repeat this pattern until you have identified the missing sentences for all the spaces.

MINI TEST 4

Read the three texts below on the theme of oceans.

Choose the option which you think best answers the question.

Which text ...

1 says changes to human behaviour can improve the health of our oceans? _____

2 gives an explanation of the origin of oceans from a scientist's point of view? _____

3 reveals the author's awe of the ocean? _____

4 implies there is more water than land on the earth's surface? _____

TEXT A

Through the open seaward door, as they sat at the table, the near sea was glimmering pale and greenish in the sunset, and breaking with a crash of foam right, as it seemed, under the house. If the house had not stood with its little grassy garden some thirty or forty feet above the ocean, sometimes the foam would have flown to the doorstep, or to the steps of the loggia. The great sea roaring at one's feet!

[...]

The waves rolled in pale and bluey, glass-green, wonderfully heavy and liquid. They curved with a long arch, then fell in a great hollow thud and a spurt of white foam and a long, soft, snow-pure rush of forward flat foam.

From *Kangaroo* by DH Lawrence

TEXT B

Where did life on earth begin? It began in the oceans. Oceans were formed billions of years ago. As far as scientists can tell, when earth was first formed it was a mass of volcanic action, molten lava, dust and rocks. As it cooled over time to below 212 degrees Fahrenheit, the boiling point of water at sea level, steam rose from the earth and formed clouds. Water condensed into rain. Rain fell from the clouds and filled deep basins of earth that is held there by gravity.

Some of the original cloud of dust and rocks, known as comets, were made of ice, some of which are still travelling around the sun. At the same time many of these comets crashed into the ground and melted. This added more water to earth. In this way, oceans were formed. They cover 70% of the earth's surface. Currently we recognise that earth has five oceans separated by continents.

TEXT C

Did you know oceans are under threat? If we don't find better ways to sustain the health of our oceans, there may be serious consequences for planet earth.

We must work at reducing our carbon footprint to help decelerate climate change. The population of the planet is getting close to 8 billion people. You can work out the maths! We should also avoid using pollutants by using non-toxic chemicals, reusable bags and cutting down on single-use plastics: straws, cutlery, containers, etc. The five trillion pieces of plastic that pollute our oceans take the lives of many precious sea creatures and damage ecosystems.

Comparing aspects of texts such as forms, structures, ideas and language use

ACTIVITY: You need to understand what each text is about and how it is written. This will enable you to compare the texts in order to choose which best provides the answer to the question.

STRATEGY: When finding which text offers the answer to a question you need to identify its subject, the view the author takes of the subject and the style used to convey its information and ideas.

TEXT A: This text describes a scene of people sitting at a table in a house set high above the ocean. The author's main focus is the ocean—what it looks like and how it moves. The beauty of its colours and the grace of its movement as the waves arc, fall and rush to the shore are described in a way that emphasises the majesty and power of the ocean.

TEXT B: This text provides a scientific explanation of how life on earth began. It begins with a question which is answered with considerable technical detail. The emphasis is on giving an accurate and full account of the sequence of events that led to the formation of oceans where it is claimed life on earth began.

TEXT C: This text is about the threat to our oceans and how we can help lessen that threat. It aims to persuade the reader to act in particular ways the author believes are important and necessary if progress is to be made. The high modality (must, should) adds an insistent tone of command to its message.

Read the text below then answer the questions.

Blue Wednesday

The first Wednesday in every month was a Perfectly Awful Day—a day to be awaited with dread, endured with courage and forgotten with haste. Every floor must be spotless, every chair dustless, and every bed without a wrinkle. Ninety-seven squirming little orphans must be scrubbed and combed and buttoned into freshly starched ginghams; and all ninety-seven reminded of their manners, and told to say, 'Yes, sir,' 'No, sir,' whenever a Trustee spoke.

It was a distressing time; and poor Jerusha Abbott, being the oldest orphan, had to bear the brunt of it. But this particular first Wednesday, like its predecessors, finally dragged itself to a close. Jerusha escaped from the pantry where she had been making sandwiches for the asylum's guests, and turned upstairs to accomplish her regular work.

[...]

The day was ended—quite successfully, so far as she knew. The Trustees and the visiting committee had made their rounds, and read their reports, and drunk their tea, and now were hurrying home to their own cheerful firesides, to forget their bothersome little charges for another month. Jerusha leaned forward watching with curiosity—and a touch of wistfulness—the stream of carriages and automobiles that rolled out of the asylum gates. In imagination she followed first one equipage, then another, to the big houses dotted along the hillside. She pictured herself in a fur coat and a velvet hat trimmed with feathers leaning back in the seat and nonchalantly murmuring 'Home' to the driver. But on the door-sill of her home the picture grew blurred ...

Je-ru-sha Ab-bott

You are want-ed

In the of-fice,

And I think you'd

Better hurry up!

Tommy Dillon, who had joined the choir, came singing up the stairs and down the corridor, his chant growing louder as he approached room F. Jerusha wrenched herself from the window and refaced the troubles of life.

'Who wants me?' she cut into Tommy's chant with a note of sharp anxiety.

Mrs Lippett's in the office,

And I think she's mad.

Ah-a-men!

[...]

Jerusha went without comment, but with two parallel lines on her brow. What could have gone wrong, she wondered.

[...]

The long lower hall had not been lighted, and as she came downstairs, a last Trustee stood, on the point of departure, in the open door that led to the porte-cochere. Jerusha caught only a fleeting impression of the man—and the impression consisted entirely of tallness. He was waving his arm towards an automobile waiting in the curved drive. As it sprang into motion and approached, head on for an instant, the glaring headlights threw his shadow sharply against the wall inside. The shadow pictured grotesquely elongated legs and arms that ran along the floor and up the wall of the corridor. It looked, for all the world, like a huge, wavering daddy-long-legs.

Jerusha's anxious frown gave place to quick laughter. She was by nature a sunny soul, and had always snatched the tiniest excuse to be amused. If one could derive any sort of entertainment out of the oppressive fact of a Trustee, it was something unexpected to the good.

[…]

'Sit down, Jerusha, I have something to say to you.' Jerusha dropped into the nearest chair and waited with a touch of breathlessness.

[…]

'To-day at the regular meeting, the question of your future was brought up.'

Mrs Lippett allowed a moment of silence to fall, then resumed in a slow, placid manner extremely trying to her hearer's suddenly tightened nerves.

[…]

'Of course the usual disposition of one in your place would be to put you in a position where you could begin to work, but you have done well in school in certain branches; it seems that your work in English has even been brilliant. Miss Pritchard, who is on our visiting committee, is also on the school board; she has been talking with your rhetoric teacher, and made a speech in your favour. She also read aloud an essay that you had written entitled, 'Blue Wednesday'.'

Jerusha's guilty expression this time was not assumed.

'It seemed to me that you showed little gratitude in holding up to ridicule the institution that has done so much for you. Had you not managed to be funny I doubt if you would have been forgiven. But fortunately for you, Mr—, that is, the gentleman who has just gone—appears to have an immoderate sense of humour. On the strength of that impertinent paper, he has offered to send you to college.'

'To college?' Jerusha's eyes grew big. Mrs Lippett nodded.

'He waited to discuss the terms with me. They are unusual. The gentleman, I may say, is erratic. He believes that you have originality, and he is planning to educate you to become a writer.'

'A writer?' Jerusha's mind was numbed. She could only repeat Mrs Lippett's words.

From *Daddy Long Legs* by Jean Webster

For questions **1–6**, choose the answer (**A, B, C** or **D**) which you think best answers the question.

1 The words 'Perfectly Awful Day' are in capitals to

   A represent how Jerusha sees the day.

   B stress the importance of the day for the Trustees.

   C exaggerate the trials the orphans have to suffer.

   D emphasise the unpleasantness of life in an orphanage.

2 What causes the images Jerusha 'sees' to suddenly become 'blurred'?

   A She is too tired to think another thought.

   B It begins to rain, which blurs the window.

   C She can't quite see herself in a home of her own.

   D Tommy distracts her from her thoughts.

3 Why are some of Tommy's words broken into syllables?

   A He has trouble getting his words out.

   B Jerusha makes him stutter.

   C He is afraid Mrs Lippett will hear him.

   D He is singing to Jerusha in a playful way.

4 Jerusha laughs suddenly because

   A it is her habit never to frown for too long.

   B the Trustee's distorted shadow makes her laugh.

   C Tommy tickles her sense of humour.

   D she imagines Mrs Lippett reading her paper.

5 What most surprises Mrs Lippett about the Trustee's offer?

   A that it proves the Trustee had a sense of humour

   B that it means Jerusha will be leaving the orphanage

   C that it is inspired by Jerusha's 'impertinent' paper

   D that Jerusha doesn't show any reaction to it

6 Mrs Lippett's tone when speaking to Jerusha is

   A quite disapproving.

   B strongly belligerent.

   C mostly threatening.

   D non-judgemental.

Read the poem below by Geoff Page then answer the questions.

For questions **7–11**, choose the answer (**A, B, C** or **D**) which you think best answers the question.

Silver Wind, my childhood mare

Silver Wind, my childhood mare,
how is it that I don't recall
the when you died, the how or where?

Your mouth was wilful to a fault;
your gait a slow resentful slouch
but you were just as keen to bolt.

I must have been at boarding school
when in some half-forgotten paddock
your hectic blood began to cool.

I like to think a vet was brought
from town to summon painlessly
the whiteness of your final thought.

Perhaps they put you on a lorry
to go where all the cattle went
or offered you the leaden *sorry*.

Your time was up. I don't know why.
Were you lame? Or too much trouble?
I doubt that I was told a lie.

Ideally, you were put to grass,
munching through a last few summers,
unconcerned to see them pass.

You taught me first what I know now
of stubbornness—and I regret
I wasn't there to see you go.

© Geoff Page; reproduced with permission

7 The poet doesn't remember

A what his horse looked like.

B anything about the death of his horse.

C anything about his horse's nature.

D what caused his horse's death.

8 Why does the poet 'like to think' of the vet being brought from town?

A He imagines the vet curing his mare's illness.

B He knows vets can tame 'hectic blood'.

C He imagines the vet giving his mare a swift, painless death.

D He knows his family always trusted their vet.

9 The poet implies his mare may have been

A shot.

B drugged.

C sent to an abattoir.

D poisoned.

10 The words 'munching through a last few summers' create a sense of

A peace.

B greed.

C distress.

D wastefulness.

11 The poet's attitude to the past in this poem is mainly

A annoyed.

B reflective.

C anxious.

D passionate.

Read the text below then answer the questions.

Six sentences have been removed from the text. Choose from the sentences (**A–G**) the one which fits each gap (**12–17**). There is one extra sentence which you do not need to use.

Lychees

Did you know that lychees are a popular fruit for celebrating Lunar New Year? **12** _____ It is celebrated around the world and is especially popular within Chinese, Vietnamese and other Asian communities.

Lychees are something many people associate with these celebrations. **13** _____ The fruit is included in celebratory meals during the Lunar Festival and given as gifts to family and friends.

Mr and Mrs Knoblock, an Australian farmer and his wife who moved from Melbourne to South Boambee on the Coffs coast, were quite unaware that lychees were part of Lunar New Year traditions. **14** _____ It was not long before they changed their minds. Why was this?

A visit from a Chinese fruit merchant alerted the Knoblocks to the fact that lychees were in high demand but not readily available in the area. This was the lucky break the family needed. They set about learning all they could about the cultivation of lychees. **15** _____ They produce five different types of lychees.

When it is time to harvest the lychees depends on many factors. **16** _____ Farms in central Queensland, for example, are likely to crop earlier than farms in New South Wales. The Knoblocks' farm is the southernmost lychee farm in Australia.

Lychee picking is popular with families. The Knoblocks encourage their visitors to hand-pick their own lychees. **17** _____ There is an entry fee but this allows pickers to eat what they want and pay only for what they take away. These days, in the lead up to the Lunar New Year, the Knoblocks say they often have busloads of people come from Sydney to get their fresh lychees.

A	When they arrived at their new home, they planned to grow snow peas.
B	This spring-time festival begins on 1 February and lasts until 15 February each year.
C	China is the main producer of lychees, followed by India and other countries in Southeast Asia.
D	These include climate and the location of the trees.
E	Today their lychee farm covers three hectares.
F	After this they weigh and pay for them.
G	It is traditional to make decorative wreaths with their branches.

SAMPLE TEST 1

Read the four texts below on the theme of stars and planets.

For questions **18–25**, choose the option (**A, B, C** or **D**) which you think best answers the question.

Which text ...

18 refers to a fictional planet? _____

19 includes a story about the stars that has a moral? _____

20 refers to scientific information about a planet that may affect earth's future? _____

21 shows behaviour on planet earth from the perspective of outsiders? _____

22 mixes scientific information about planets with personal comments? _____

23 reveals links between ancient and modern cultures? _____

24 is sceptical about the information on the influence of stars on human lives? _____

25 includes scientific information about the planets learned from private study? _____

TEXT A

Aboriginal and/or Torres Strait Islander peoples have a long tradition of observing the stars. They have used their observations to navigate the Australian landscape for tens of thousands of years. Their star maps are memorised in song and passed on to others. Research has revealed that when some Aboriginal star maps are lined up with modern road maps, there is often overlap. This is less surprising when you recall that many early explorers used First Australians as guides. Many of these same routes became tracks and eventually roads and highways.

The stars also play a part in First Nations belief systems. They are seen as the homes of ancestors, animals, plants and spirits. The Dhui Dhui story of the Bandjin people, for example, records how two boys disobeyed a warning from their elders and ended up in the sky! They were told not to fish from their canoe at a sand spit where a dangerous Dhui Dhui (shovelnose ray) lived. The ray bit their line and hung on to it but the boys wouldn't let go. They were towed away until they disappeared. That night their families saw the Southern Cross rising and recognized the Dhui Dhui and the two Pointer stars—the boys in their canoe.

TEXT B

Astrologers believe that at particular times the position of heavenly bodies such as stars influence human affairs. They claim that the time of your birth, for example, has an impact on your personality type. They provide their predictions about the kind of influence the stars exert in horoscopes or charts that make popular inclusions in newspapers and magazines. People like to read their 'stars' to see what is likely to happen in their lives in a particular time period. No scientific studies have shown there is any accuracy in these predictions.

Twelve zodiac signs that correspond to the position of the sun at particular times in the calendar year are recognised and grouped as signs that link to fire, earth, air and water.

TEXT C

I can highly recommend *Halfway Across the Galaxy and Turn Left*, a novel by the Australian author Robin Klein. The story is about a family of aliens from the planet Zyrgon who escape to Bellwood, a town on earth. They are fleeing from the galactic police, known as The Law-Enforcers.

The police want to capture Mortimer, a gambler, who had become very successful at cheating at the government lotteries. His youngest daughter, X, is in charge of the family as her mother prefers it that way. (X's responsibilities weigh on her so heavily they eventually make her ill.) The other children include Dovis, a cosmic flier, and Qwrk, a young genius.

Finding ways to fit in on earth is not easy for the family. This is partly because Zyrgonians are so different from humans and have unusual abilities such as being able to levitate. It is also because they find the ways people on earth choose to live unsettling. For example, they find the concept of having to go to school extraordinarily unpleasant! However, in time, most of them come to love planet earth.

TEXT D

Dear Riley

You asked me what I'd been doing in lockdown. I've been studying some astronomy. It is mind-blowing to get your head around, especially when you consider the time and distances involved.

Did you know that the planet, Pluto, is 5.8 billion kilometres from the sun and takes 248 years to complete its orbit around it? It has the coldest atmosphere of any of the planets: the temperature there is minus 238 °C. In contrast, Venus is the hottest planet. Its atmosphere is over 400 °C (no air conditioning as far as I know).

Mars, 228 million kilometres from the sun, is currently of great interest to scientists. Its temperature is not as extreme as that of other planets. It is viewed as the only planet humans might, one day, be able to inhabit. In 2020 NASA sent a mobile laboratory, the Perseverance Rover, to Mars, to carry out experiments there (no meetings with Martians reported so far).

What have you and the family been up to in your lockdown time?

Love
Gran

Read the text below then answer the questions.

Mowgli returns

Mowgli was separated from his human family as a baby and raised by wolves in the jungle.

He hurried on, keeping to the rough road that ran down the valley, and followed it at a steady jog-trot for nearly twenty miles, till he came to a country that he did not know. The valley opened out into a great plain dotted over with rocks and cut up by ravines. At one end stood a little village, and at the other the thick jungle came down in a sweep to the grazing-grounds, and stopped there as though it had been cut off with a hoe. All over the plain, cattle and buffaloes were grazing, and when the little boys in charge of the herds saw Mowgli they shouted and ran away, and the yellow pariah dogs that hang about every Indian village barked. Mowgli walked on, for he was feeling hungry.

[...]

He sat down by the gate, and when a man came out he stood up, opened his mouth, and pointed down it to show that he wanted food. The man stared, and ran back up the one street of the village shouting for the priest, who was a big, fat man dressed in white, with a red and yellow mark on his forehead. The priest came to the gate, and with him at least a hundred people, who stared and talked and shouted and pointed at Mowgli.

'They have no manners, these Men Folk,' said Mowgli to himself. 'Only the grey ape would behave as they do.' So he threw back his long hair and frowned at the crowd.

'What is there to be afraid of?' said the priest. 'Look at the marks on his arms and legs. They are the bites of wolves. He is but a wolf-child run away from the jungle.'

Of course, in playing together, the cubs had often nipped Mowgli harder than they intended, and there were white scars all over his arms and legs. But he would have been the last person in the world to call these bites, for he knew what real biting meant.

'Arre! Arre!' said two or three women together. 'To be bitten by wolves, poor child! He is a handsome boy. He has eyes like red fire. By my honor, Messua, he is not unlike thy boy that was taken by the tiger.'

'Let me look,' said a woman with heavy copper rings on her wrists and ankles, and she peered at Mowgli under the palm of her hand. 'Indeed he is not. He is thinner, but he has the very look of my boy.'

The priest was a clever man, and he knew that Messua was wife to the richest villager in the place. So he looked up at the sky for a minute and said solemnly: 'What the jungle has taken the jungle has restored. Take the boy into thy house, my sister, and forget not to honor the priest who sees so far into the lives of men.'

'By the Bull that bought me,' said Mowgli to himself, 'but all this talking is like another looking-over by the Pack! Well, if I am a man, a man I must become.'

The crowd parted as the woman beckoned Mowgli to her hut.

[...]

She gave him a long drink of milk and some bread, and then she laid her hand on his head and looked into his eyes; for she thought perhaps that he might be her real son come back from the jungle where the tiger had taken him. So she said, 'Nathoo, O Nathoo!' Mowgli did not show that he knew the name. 'Dost thou not remember the day when I gave thee thy new shoes?' She touched his foot, and it was almost as hard as horn. 'No,' she said sorrowfully, 'those feet have never worn shoes, but thou art very like my Nathoo, and thou shalt be my son.'

Mowgli was uneasy, because he had never been under a roof before. But as he looked at the thatch, he saw that he could tear it out any time if he wanted to get away, and that the window had no fastenings. 'What is the good of a man,' he said to himself at last, 'if he does not understand man's talk? Now I am as silly and dumb as a man would be with us in the jungle. I must speak their talk.'

It was not for fun that he had learned while he was with the wolves to imitate the challenge of bucks in the jungle and the grunt of the little wild pig. So, as soon as Messua pronounced a word Mowgli would imitate it almost perfectly, and before dark he had learned the names of many things in the hut.

From *The Jungle Book* by Rudyard Kipling

For questions **1–6**, choose the answer (**A, B, C** or **D**) which you think best answers the question.

1 How does the reader know Mowgli looks different from other boys?

A He can jog-trot for very long distances.

B He doesn't use human language.

C Boys run away from their work when they see him.

D He frowns at everyone.

2 The main reason the priest tells Messua to take Mowgli into her house is that the priest

A sees a way to make money from Messua.

B wants Messua to get over her sorrow.

C believes Mowgli is Messua's son stolen by a tiger.

D sees far into the lives of men.

3 Mowgli thinks the crowd

A is threatening.

B behaves in an ill-mannered way.

C is scarier than a pack of wolves.

D would be easy to attack.

4 What mainly convinces Messua that Mowgli is not her son?

A the scars on his arms

B the skinniness of his body

C the look in his eyes

D the hardness of his feet

5 What does Mowgli see that encourages him to stay with Messua?

A the valuable copper rings and bracelets on her arms

B plenty of milk and bread

C the loving expression on Messua's face

D roof thatch he could tear away and a window he could escape through

6 Mowgli recognises staying with Messua will give him the advantage of

A escaping from the wolves.

B earning the favour of the priest.

C learning the language of men.

D belonging to a wealthy villager.

Read the poem below by Donna Gibbs then answer the questions.

What's in a Name?

What's in a name?
The trouble is
I don't like my name.
I'm just not that person.
I can't blame my parents—
they didn't know how I'd turn out.

The night before I was born
my mum was at the movies
watching a starlet.
A popular pin-up girl,
wholesome and beautiful.

Maybe that's how she hoped I'd be.
It probably felt right at the time
and I suppose you could call me wholesome.

I google my starlet to see if she used her real
    name.
No! Some publicity guy gave it to her
and, she added, she'd never liked the name.
She said it had 'a cold, forbidding sound'.
So there!

Anyway, I'm about to start at a new school
and ... this is my big chance.
'I'm Ash. What's your name?' the girl asks.
I try to stutter out my new name,
I'd settled on Skye,
but then I blush and in a rush
I swallow it down.
I tell her my real name.

© Donna Gibbs; reproduced with permission

For questions **7–11**, choose the answer (**A, B, C** or **D**) which you think best answers the question.

7 Which line offers an excuse for her parents' choice of name?

  A I'm just not that person.

  B my mum was at the movies

  C It probably felt right at the time

  D and I suppose you could call me wholesome.

8 The main reason the narrator dislikes her name is

  A she didn't want to be named after a movie star.

  B she doesn't identify with the name.

  C she feels her parents were punishing her.

  D she thinks she isn't beautiful enough for it.

9 The word 'google' tells us the narrator is

  A an old-fashioned girl.

  B a technological whiz-kid.

  C a competent internet user.

  D a show-off.

10 How would you describe the tone of the poem?

  A formal

  B childish

  C angry

  D conversational

11 What stops the narrator from saying her new name?

  A She is embarrassed by the name she has chosen.

  B She can't bring herself to say something that isn't true.

  C She decides she prefers the name she has.

  D She is confused about what to say.

SAMPLE TEST 2

Read the text below then answer the questions.

Six sentences have been removed from the text. Choose from the sentences (**A–G**) the one which fits each gap (**12–17**). There is one extra sentence which you do not need to use.

Tattoos

Human beings have used tattoos on their bodies as far back as history records. Tattoos are marks or images added to the skin. **12** _____ Tattoos can also be put on the skin by using materials that leave no permanent mark.

The designs people choose vary enormously. Some are geometric designs (lines, zigzags, repeating shapes); others involve stylised representations of animals, plants or humans. **13** _____ They can be used, for example, for decoration, for spiritual purposes, to display connections between family members or particular groups, for self-expression or as a status symbol.

Traditional sailor tattoos provided a way to communicate information about status and experiences at sea. **14** _____ A tattoo of a full-rigged ship confirmed a sailor has sailed around Cape Horn; a shell-back turtle showed that the Equator has been crossed. Each tattoo of a swallow on a sailor indicated the achievement of sailing 5000 nautical miles.

Sometimes sailors chose tattoos for superstitious reasons. Tattoos of roosters and pigs inked onto their feet were thought to keep them safe during a shipwreck. **15** _____ It was seen as a symbol of hope that a sailor would find his way home. Since before modern navigation systems were in use, sailors were dependent on their knowledge of the stars for navigation purposes so this belief is unsurprising.

In some cultures, tattoos are frowned upon. **16** _____ This is probably because, in the past, Japanese criminals were tattooed for their offences and the sense of taboo has lingered.

In modern societies, tattoos have gained in popularity for decoration or self-expression. **17** _____ However, temporary tattoos are also becoming increasingly popular as people recognise that, as they age, they may change their mind about what they want to have permanently on their bodies.

A	In Japan, for example, at least until recently, people have been banned from beaches, swimming pools and other public areas if they wear body art.
B	A star was also worn for superstitious reasons.
C	This can be done through inserting dye or ink in a way that leaves a permanent mark or pattern.
D	The purposes for which they are used within a culture also vary.
E	This popularity has been encouraged by social media where celebrities, athletes and others sport them in public view.
F	Inuit women used needles made of bone or sinew soaked in suet to tattoo their bodies.
G	A boatswain, for example, wore crossed anchors on the webbing between thumb and index finger to indicate status.

Read the four texts below on the theme of speed.

For questions **18–25**, choose the option (**A, B, C** or **D**) which you think best answers the question.

Which text ...

18 shows respect for what scientists are able to do in relation to speed? _____

19 is a spoken text about speed (that has been written down)? _____

20 gives examples of speed records as part of biographical information? _____

21 draws a moral related to speed? _____

22 is most likely to be found in a section on speed in a science textbook? _____

23 suggests that research into movement in animals could lead to helping humans in the future? _____

24 mentions personal information? _____

25 includes an animal that makes judgements related to speed? _____

TEXT A

We are sad to say the Australian tiger beetle has lost its crown as the king of speed in the bug kingdom. For some time now the tiger beetle has held the record for running at a speed measured by body lengths per second. It is claimed the tiger beetle reaches a speed of 171 body lengths per second. But new research by a team studying biology in Claremont, California, claims the speed of the Californian mite blows that record out of the water.

The mite is very small, about the size of a large grain of sand, and it can run twice as fast as a tiger beetle. The researchers clocked mites running at a speed of up to 322 body lengths per second. That is the same as a human running at about 2 100 km per hour.

More research into the way these animals move may provide useful information for understanding how better to design products that could be helpful to humans. Robots come to mind. And now to the weather.

TEXT B

Speed is the rate or rapidity at which something or someone moves. It is a scalar quality (scalars describe a numerical value) that measures how fast an object moves in relation to distance covered. Something that moves quickly and covers a large distance in a short amount of time is said to have a high speed. The cheetah, for example, can reach speeds of up to 113 km per hour. Something that moves slowly and covers a small distance in a similar time frame is said to have a low speed. The sea anemone, for example, moves at a pace of around one centimetre per hour.

Scientists are able to accurately measure very different things, such as the speed of light, the speed of wind, the speed of sound or the speed at which a flower unfolds. Measuring these different things can be complex tasks and often require highly specialised equipment.

TEXT C

The Hare was much amused at the idea of running a race with the Tortoise, but for the fun of the thing he agreed. So the Fox, who had consented to act as judge, marked the distance and started the runners off.

The Hare was soon far out of sight, and to make the Tortoise feel very deeply how ridiculous it was for him to try a race with a Hare, he lay down beside the course to take a nap until the Tortoise should catch up.

The Tortoise meanwhile kept going slowly but steadily, and, after a time, passed the place where the Hare was sleeping. But the Hare slept on very peacefully; and when at last he did wake up, the Tortoise was near the goal. The Hare now ran his swiftest, but he could not overtake the Tortoise in time.

TEXT D

Usain St Leo Bolt is thought by many to be the greatest sprinter of all time. He was born in a small village in Jamaica in 1986 and says that as a child he didn't think of much else than playing sports. By the time he was twelve, he was his school's fastest runner in the 100 metres. He was later to win this race at the 2009 Olympics in the world record time of 9.58 seconds, the fastest time this race has ever been run.

Bolt has won gold at the Olympics on eight occasions and has been the most successful male athlete at the World Championships. He won the 100 and 200 metres at three consecutive Olympics. The 2008 Olympic golds he won for the 100 and 200 metres were both run in world-record times; in fact, he has broken his own world records on several occasions.

Since retiring Bolt has co-founded an electric scooter company and has worked as a dancehall music producer. He and his partner have a daughter named Olympia Lightning Bolt and twin sons named Saint Leo and Thunder.

Read the text below then answer the questions.

Pocket of Secrets

Sam was too nervous to try again. He was dead scared of what his dad would do if he discovered he'd meddled with his precious Aviator. But I'd thought and thought about what Sam had told me. It must be that you controlled the Aviator with your mind—not knobs or buttons but the power of your mind. That's how Sam got back from the past; he'd wanted to be at home again very badly. If I could work out how to focus my mind on the time and place where I wanted to be, the Aviator would take me there.

[...]

The whole thing happened exactly as Sam had described. I used the combinations to get everything unlocked and attached the cables of the Aviator into the slots on the computer, then linked it into the program. Trying not to think about what might happen to my body, I stared into the dish. My reverse image multiplied and tiny replicas of me, Kate Dower, began their march into the darkness, just as Sam said his had done. I was on track.

The beauty of the bubbles as they formed held me spellbound. Other spherical shapes were spinning inside the main bubble-like projection and when I looked closely, I could see people's faces and different landscapes swirling past. It was as if other times and places were circling each other. I guessed that Sam had been too obsessed with the patterns that were made to see what was before him.

As I felt my body slip away, I lost concentration. Not such a good idea! I'd meant to focus my mind on a particular time and place where my grandmother might have been but I found all I could think of was going on the journey. I stared at what was passing before me and as I did so an image of the bushranger, Ned Kelly, drifted uninvited into my mind. A patch of brightness separated itself from the patterns in red and black moving behind the curtains of my eyelids. I was on my way, but to where?

****

Stretches of empty grey-green land, clumps of tall gum trees, strips of bark lying lazily about, flies buzzing. Looking down I found I was dressed in a long dark-blue cotton dress tied at the back with a sash of the same material. Black laced boots instead of my old sneakers. Where had my jeans and t-shirt gone? There was something underneath my dress—bony sorts of things that made me feel like a trussed-up parcel. Snatches of laughter, voices shouting and every now and then the drumming of horses' hooves. The cracking of a whip. Or was it a gunshot?

To the left, down a winding track I saw a gate made from grey logs bound roughly together. A wooden plank swung from a lintel over the gate with the words *Faithfull's Creek Station* burnt deeply into its wood. The property looked as if it had been fenced quite recently. Well, recently a long time ago, if you know what I mean.

Lifting the semi-circular tin catch that kept the gate closed, I followed the drive for nearly a kilometre. I was getting hotter by the minute in my unaccustomed clothing. The only good thing about these tight, constricting undergarments was the little waist they gave me. I kept spanning it with both my hands just to check.

A bush picnic. So that was the source of the noise. People sat in groups on the ground, cheerfully eating and drinking while others were seated on the wide verandah of the homestead some distance away. In a roped off-corral, eyes were drawn to the trick riding and fancy footwork of two young cowboys. I moved to a space in the crowd, not far from two men who stood a little apart, talking softly together.

'That was a fair haul from the bank, Ned. The manager's face when you shoved all them mortgage records in the fire was priceless. What next?'

Ned! And a bank robbery. It had to be Ned Kelly! I recalled now it was only this morning that Ms Hooper had shown our class pictures of Ned Kelly and told us about the Kelly Gang's famous robbery of December 1878.

'The manager and his buddies are tied up now in the front room with the others at the Station. When we go, we'll warn them we want three hours to get away. If they go to the police in less than that, we'll be back for 'em.'

'That's it, Ned. Are you gonna show us your riding tricks now before we head off?'

'Yep. My turn next with Dan and Steve.'

He turned towards his horse, brushing past me.

Warm, bright eyes you could swim in. For a moment, I felt quite dizzy. My 'new' corset must be affecting me!

'Watch it Blondie,' he said, reaching out to steady me. 'Get this girl some water,' Ned called to a young woman who had been standing near him. Then, leaping into the saddle, he turned his horse's head towards the corral.

From *Pocket of Secrets* by Donna Gibbs
© Donna Gibbs; reproduced with permission

For questions **1–6**, choose the answer (**A, B, C** or **D**) which you think best answers the question.

1 The Aviator is most likely to be

A a new form of public transport.

B a type of time machine.

C a very modern aeroplane.

D a robot that can cover vast distances.

2 The problem Kate sees with losing concentration is that she could

A lose control over where she wants to go.

B forget how to follow the instructions on the machine.

C be caught by Sam's father and handed over to the police.

D end up trapped in the machine forever.

3 The genre of this story can best be described as

A mystery.

B fantasy.

C crime.

D romance.

4 To when and where does Kate travel?

A 20th-century urban Australia

B the 19th century; an unidentified setting

C the 19th century; rural Victoria

D the 18th century; rural New South Wales

5 On the whole, Kate's narrative voice tends to be

A impersonal.

B conversational.

C judgemental.

D humorous.

6 The most likely reason Ned Kelly suggests Kate be given some water is that

A he wants her to feel grateful to him.

B he thought she had mesmerising eyes.

C he wants to draw attention to himself.

D she looks as if she might faint.

Read the poem below by Alfred Lord Tennyson then answer the questions.

The Brook

I come from haunts of coot* and hern*,
I make a sudden sally
And sparkle out among the fern,
To bicker down a valley.
By thirty hills I hurry down,
Or slip between the ridges,
By twenty thorps**, a little town,
And half a hundred bridges.

I chatter over stony ways,
In little sharps and trebles,
I bubble into eddying bays,
I babble on the pebbles.
With many a curve my banks I fret
By many a field and fallow,
And many a fairy foreland set
With willow-weed and mallow.

And here and there a foamy lake
Upon me, as I travel
With many a silvery waterbreak
Above the golden gravel,
And draw them all along, and flow
To join the brimming river,
For men may come and men may go,
But I go on for ever.

*water birds **little villages

For questions **7–11**, choose the answer (**A, B, C** or **D**) which you think best answers the question.

7 The speaking voice of the poem belongs to
  A the poet.
  B the brook.
  C the natural world.
  D humankind.

8 The brook moves
  A swiftly forward without pause.
  B in a meandering, gentle way.
  C slowly through the landscape.
  D at varying speeds according to what it encounters.

9 The 'little sharps and trebles' referred to are
  A groups of stones.
  B music being played nearby.
  C the musical sounds of the brook.
  D the bird sounds made by coot and hern.

10 The brook's voice is
  A sad and wistful.
  B lively and triumphant.
  C comical.
  D aggressive.

11 The brook sees itself as
  A having an advantage over all of nature.
  B being less important than the river.
  C having an advantage over humankind.
  D being less important than the lake.

Read the text below then answer the questions.

Six sentences have been removed from the text. Choose from the sentences (**A–G**) the one which fits each gap (**12–17**). There is one extra sentence which you do not need to use.

Merpeople

Merpeople, or merfolk, are water-dwelling beings who often feature in myths and legends from cultures around the world. **12** _____ There are similar words for sea in French (*mer*), Italian and Spanish (*mare*), and so on.

Examples of merpeople include mermaids—beings who are part woman, part fish—and mermen—beings who are part man, part fish. **13** _____ Selkies, beings who change from seal to human by shedding their skin, can live on both land and sea.

Throughout the ages people have told stories about merpeople. One of the earliest references to a merperson was to a sea god in the 3rd century BCE. **14** _____ Ea was said to have had a fish's head with a man's head beneath, and both a fish's tail and a man's legs.

Medieval Chinese stories include creatures such as the *jiaoren* (flood dragon or shark people). **15** _____ When the silk spinners 'cry', pearls—not tears—are said to fall from their eyes.

In the 18th century there was a growing belief that these fantastical creatures were real. **16** _____ Eyewitness accounts came from groups of fishermen who swore they had seen mermaids or mermen.

In modern times, scientists are highly sceptical that such creatures exist. **17** _____ For example, think of the terrifying mermaids in *The Pirates of the Caribbean* or those who appear in the Narnia and Harry Potter stories.

A   Some of these Chinese legendary figures live under water, like fish, but spend their time weaving and spinning silk.

B   Many travellers reported seeing examples of them in captivity.

C   The word mer, or mere, is the old-English word for sea.

D   Berossus, a priest and astronomer, wrote about Ea, the early Babylonian sea god.

E   Mermaids are often associated with misfortune and death.

F   These creatures live in the sea and are not able to survive on land.

G   Even so, merpeople are commonly included in literature, film and other types of popular culture.

SAMPLE TEST 3

Read the four texts below on the theme of size.

For questions **18–25**, choose the option (**A, B, C** or **D**) which you think best answers the question.

Which text ...

18   refers to practices related to size in previous centuries?   _____

19   refers to a range of places that use size as an attraction?   _____

20   uses a synonym for the word big?   _____

21   changes the case of words to represent their meanings?   _____

22   implies matters of size can be out of human control?   _____

23   includes a girl and an animal that are roughly the same size?   _____

24   invites an audience to respond to a message about oversized objects?   _____

25   includes a definition of something related to size that is popular with adults
and children?   _____

TEXT A

Now, though Goldilocks did not know it, this house belonged to three bears. There was a GREAT
BIG FATHER BEAR, and a MIDDLING-SIZED MOTHER BEAR, and a *dear little baby bear*, no bigger
than Goldilocks herself. But the three bears had gone out to take a walk in the forest while their
supper was cooling, so when Goldilocks knocked at the door no one answered her.

She waited awhile and then she knocked again, and as still nobody answered her, she pushed the
door open and stepped inside. There in a row stood three chairs. One was a GREAT BIG CHAIR,
and it belonged to the father bear. And one was a MIDDLING-SIZED CHAIR, and it belonged to the
mother bear, and one was a *dear little chair*, and it belonged to the baby bear. And on the table stood
three bowls of smoking hot porridge. 'And so,' thought Goldilocks, 'the people must be coming back
soon to eat it.'

She thought she would sit down and rest until they came.

[...]

Then she sat down in the *dear little chair*, and it was just right. So there she sat, and she rocked and she
rocked, and she sat and she sat, until with her rocking and her sitting she sat the bottom right out of it.

From 'Goldilocks and the Three Bears' in *Mother's Nursery Tales* by Katherine Pyle

---

TEXT B

Australia loves its series of 'Big' sculptures dotted around the countryside. Some of you are sure to have heard of, or visited, the Big Banana in Coffs Harbour, New South Wales, the Big Pineapple on the Sunshine Coast, Queensland, or the Big Orange on the Harvey River, Western Australia. Other 'Big' icons include the Big Cane Toad (nicknamed Buffy), the Big Merino, the Big Lobster, the Big Potato, the Big Platypus and the Big Dead Fish.

You will notice most of the objects chosen to be given 'Big' status tend to be animals or fruit. There's a good explanation for this. They often represent things that are important to the local area or are examples of local produce. They are icons that serve to attract tourists and bring money into the local community.

Some describe our 'Big' objects as a quirky national obsession that will never end. Others think it is a trend that has had its day. What do you think? Send your thoughts to us at <u>www.thebigblogspot.com.au</u>.

TEXT C

A miniature is a representation or image of anything on a very small scale. People are attracted to miniatures for many reasons and they are popular with collectors.

In the 16th and 17th centuries, a miniature home was often kept in the main room of a wealthy person's home to display the owner's collection of expensive miniature objects. In some of these households, it also served as a visual aid for children being taught the skills to manage a large household. In the 18th century the 'baby house' arrived. It was a replica of an owner's home and furniture rather than a storehouse for valuable miniature objects. It wasn't until the 20th century, when objects were mass produced, that doll's houses became more affordable and were specifically made for children to play with.

Tiny replicas of people, animals and objects have been created for different purposes throughout history. Miniature replicas of military figures, for example, are put on display in people's homes and in museums, or may be used to recreate actual battles that have taken place. Children love to collect miniature replicas such as cars, dinosaurs, farm animals and even imaginary monsters.

TEXT D

A tsunami is a large, often destructive, sea wave caused by an underwater earthquake. It is not surprising to find the name comes from the Japanese words *tsu* (harbour) and *nami* (wave), as Japan has suffered from the devastating effect of tsunamis on many occasions.

Tsunamis also occur fairly regularly in Australia, although they have not caused the largescale destruction that has occurred in some countries. In 2006 an earthquake near Java, Indonesia, measuring 7.7 on the Richter scale, caused a tsunami that flooded a campsite at Steep Point, Western Australia. In 2022 the eruption of an underwater volcano in Tonga caused a tsunami felt across the Pacific Ocean which reached Australia. The waves that arrived here were comparable to some of the biggest tsunami waves Australia has ever recorded.

Documenting the pattern and behaviour of tsunamis helps prepare us for future tsunamis. Even so, this knowledge doesn't help us predict how big these might be. That, as they say, is in the lap of the gods.

Read the text below then answer the questions.

Blueback by Tim Winton

That summer, as his skill and confidence grew, Abel took his boat up and down the coast exploring the long lonely stretches that made him feel small. Land and sea were so big he became dizzy just imagining how far they went. He felt like a speck, like a bubble on the sea left by a breaking wave, here for a moment and then gone. He pulled into tiny sheltered coves and swam with his mother in turquoise water beneath streaky cliffs and trees loud with birds. Some days he sped close in to long sugary beaches. He stayed just behind the breakers and was showered with their spray and saw the great, strange land through the wobbly glass of the waves. He saw the sun melting like butter on white dunes. Dolphins rose in his bow wave and he slapped them playfully with his rolled up towel. He drifted amidst huge schools of tuna as they rose around him, feeding like packs of wild dogs on terrified baitfish that leapt across his boat.

Some days out east, he saw a big red jet boat working its way along the coast with its dive flags streaming.

'Costello,' said his mother. 'The abalone diver. He's a hard case.'

'He'll be here soon,' said Abel.

'I know,' said his mother.

'What about Blueback*?'

'It's not just Blueback I'm worried about,' said his mother. 'It's the whole bay. People say he takes everything he sees.'

'So what do we do?'

'Nothing. We stay out of his way.'

'But Mum, what about Blueback?'

'He'll have to look after himself.'

'Can't we keep this bloke out of the bay?'

'This patch of land's ours, Abel. But the water belongs to everybody. Costello has a licence to take abalone. There's nothing we can do about it."

'Can't someone stop him?'

'Only the Fisheries Department. They've been watching him.'

'But out here he can get away with anything, Mum. This is the middle of nowhere.'

Abel looked across the moving water. He knew that when the time came he wouldn't just do nothing. He couldn't do nothing. ·

Abel swam with Blueback every chance he had. He tempted him with squid and cray legs. He felt the broad blade of the fish's tail against his chest and touched those flat white teeth with his fingertips. Abel held his breath and stared into the groper's face trying to read it. Blueback swam down to his crack in the reef and looked out with moon eyes.

It was dawn when Abel heard the jet motor burbling into Long Bay. He climbed out of bed and found his way to the verandah. His mother was already there. The red boat slid in around the point and drifted with its motor off. An anchor splashed in the quiet. Then the compressor started up and two divers went over the side.

Abel's mother watched through binoculars.

'Things aren't the same, Abel. It's getting harder to hold on to the good things.'

'Let's go out and cut his hoses,' said Abel.

'Don't talk like that.'

'Well, we have to stop him somehow.'

'We don't know that he's doing anything wrong.'

'And what happens when he starts doing wrong?'

She sighed. They went indoors.

At breakfast Abel's mother looked sad and thoughtful. All these holidays he'd been feeling bigger and older. Now that he looked properly he saw that his mother was ageing too. It was a surprise. To him she had always seemed the same age. In a year or so he'd be as tall as her.

'I've been wondering,' she said. 'Do you think I should sell up?'

Abel was speechless.

*The Blueback of the book's title is a huge old groper fish.

From *Blueback* by Tim Winton

© Tim Winton; reproduced with permission from Penguin Random House

For questions **1–6**, choose the answer (**A, B, C** or **D**) which you think best answers the question.

1   Why does Abel feel small and 'like a bubble on the sea' when he is exploring in his boat?

   A He is not yet adult sized.

   B The natural world is so vast he feels dwarfed by it.

   C He likes to think of himself as part of the sea.

   D The glass of the waves magnifies the world around him.

2   Abel's mother says they should do 'Nothing' because she

   A doesn't care anymore about what happens.

   B believes Blueback will be able to look after himself.

   C is afraid Costello will harm Abel.

   D believes they have no legal right to do anything.

3   The relationship between Abel and his mother is

   A distant.

   B suffocating.

   C close.

   D stand-offish.

4   The main reason Abel and his mother fear Costello is because he

   A is an abalone diver.

   B takes everything he sees.

   C has a jet boat.

   D has a licence.

5   The author implies Abel's relationship with Blueback is

   A devoted and special.

   B typical and unsurprising.

   C thoughtless and carefree.

   D meaningless and destructive.

6   Abel was 'speechless' because he

   A couldn't believe he hadn't thought of this solution for himself.

   B realised his mother's plan would save them.

   C realised his mother had been deceiving him about her love of the bay.

   D was horrified by his mother's question.

Read the poem below by Lewis Carroll then answer the questions.

Father William

'You are old, Father William,' the young man said,
'And your hair has become very white;
And yet you incessantly stand on your head—
Do you think, at your age, it is right?'

'In my youth,' Father William replied to his son,
'I feared it might injure the brain;
But now that I'm perfectly sure I have none,
Why, I do it again and again.'

'You are old,' said the youth, 'as I mentioned before,
And have grown most uncommonly fat;
Yet you turned a back-somersault in at the door—
Pray, what is the reason of that?'

'In my youth,' said the sage, as he shook his gray
    locks,
'I kept all my limbs very supple
By the use of this ointment—one shilling the box—
Allow me to sell you a couple.'

'You are old,' said the youth, 'and your jaws are
    too weak
For anything tougher than suet;
Yet you finished the goose, with the bones and the
    beak:
Pray, how did you manage to do it?'

'In my youth,' said his father, 'I took to the law,
And argued each case with my wife;
And the muscular strength which it gave to my jaw
Has lasted the rest of my life.'

'You are old,' said the youth; 'one would hardly
    suppose
That your eye was as steady as ever;
Yet you balanced an eel on the end of your nose—
What made you so awfully clever?'

'I have answered three questions, and that is enough,'
Said his father, 'don't give yourself airs!
Do you think I can listen all day to such stuff?
Be off, or I'll kick you down-stairs!'

For questions **7–11**, choose the answer (**A**, **B**, **C** or **D**) which you think best answers the question.

7 The poem is structured as

A a narrative.

B a dialogue.

C a series of memories.

D a monologue.

8 What image does the son project of his father?

A a foolish, fat old man

B a successful person

C a fount of wisdom

D kindly but forgetful

9 In which stanza does the father explain why he did so well in his career?

A stanza 2

B stanza 4

C stanza 6

D stanza 8

10 The poem treats the generation gap

A seriously.

B wisely.

C sympathetically.

D comically.

11 The last verse differs in form from the earlier verses because

A the father loses the plot.

B the son asks his question differently.

C the father alters the pattern of his reply to end the conversation.

D the poet wants to vary the rhyme scheme.

Read the text below then answer the questions.

Six sentences have been removed from the text. Choose from the sentences (**A–G**) the one which fits each gap (**12–17**). There is one extra sentence which you do not need to use.

Woollarawarre Bennelong

Woollarawarre Bennelong (c. 1764–1813) belonged to the Eora Nation. **12** _____ He grew up near the Parramatta River where he learned to gather oysters, catch fish with a muting (spear) and make a nawi (canoe) from stringy bark.

It is thought that Bennelong had at least four sisters. **13** _____ This gave Bennelong helpful political links he could call upon when needed. He also had several wives. **14** _____ Next he married Barangaroo, a Cammeray woman. After her death, he is said to have kidnapped Kurubarabula, a Gweagal woman. They stayed together until he went to England.

In 1788 Governor Arthur Philip had two First Australians kidnapped so he could learn more about them. One of them escaped; the other was Bennelong. **15** _____ Later he chose to live in a brick hut built for him by Philip at Bennelong Point (Jubgalee), a well-known gathering place for the Eora peoples, and where the Opera House now stands.

Bennelong learnt English and was a helpful source of information for Philip about his people, their ways and their language. In 1792 he sailed to England with Philip where, dressed in his famous spotted waistcoat and ruffled shirt, he attended plays at Covent Garden and sessions at the Houses of Parliament. **16** _____ Eventually he grew homesick and in 1795 returned to Sydney on *HMS Reliance* in very poor health.

In 1796 Bennelong wrote a letter to Mr and Mrs Phillips with whom he had stayed for some time when he was in England. **17** _____ This is the first known text written in English by a First Nations Australian.

He was killed in a tribal fight in 1813 and buried in Western Sydney in the orchard of the brewer James Squire, a firm friend of Bennelong and his people.

A The first, whose name is no longer known, died, probably from smallpox.

B He lived for a time in an upstairs room in Governor Philip's house, bringing his wife, Barangaroo, to visit.

C They married important men from nearby nations.

D As a sign of kinship, he gave Philip the Aboriginal name, Wolawaree.

E When the British arrived in Australia in 1788, these people lived in the Port Jackson area.

F He thanked them for caring for him and also asked them to send him stockings and a handkerchief.

G He visited St Paul's Cathedral and the Tower of London.

Read the four texts below on the theme of birth.

For questions **18–25**, choose the option (**A, B, C** or **D**) which you think best answers the question.

Which text ...

18   refers to a type of birth that is unique in the animal kingdom?   _____

19   includes the most technical detail of a birth?   _____

20   mentions a newborn animal that is larger than a jellybean?   _____

21   would not be included in a science textbook about birth?   _____

22   describes the lengthiest birth process?   _____

23   exaggerates how quickly the newborn develops?   _____

24   refers to a place of safety for its newborn to develop?   _____

25   includes a scientific theory about a particular behaviour related to birth?   _____

TEXT A

Did you know that giraffes give birth standing up? They have a long pregnancy of around a year and a quarter. When the baby is about to be born, the giraffe stands to push the baby calf out of its body. This helps protect its long neck. Its fall to the ground doesn't hurt and it aids the breaking of its umbilical cord. The shock of the fall also helps the baby giraffe take its first breath. At birth a calf is about 1.8 metres tall and is able to stand, feed and move around. By the time the calf turns one, it will have doubled in size. These are important abilities to have in its habitat in the wild where hungry predators lurk.

Did you know that it is the male seahorse who gives birth to its babies? Seahorses and their relatives are the only species where this happens. After a long courtship, the female seahorse leaves her bright orange-coloured eggs in the male's brood pouch. After about three weeks, up to 2000 tiny baby seahorses, each about the size of a jelly bean, will be born. Very few of these are likely to survive. Scientists suggest the males of the fish family to which seahorses belong have evolved as the birth parent because it frees the female to make more eggs. This means the species can create babies quickly which is essential for its survival.

TEXT B

Marsupials, such as kangaroos, wallabies, wombats and koalas, carry their babies in a pouch. In fact the word marsupial comes from *marsupium*, the technical word for the abdominal pouch.

A baby kangaroo, or joey as it is called, spends about a month in its mother's womb before it is born. It then leaves the birth canal near its mother's tail and crawls into her pouch. Its forelimbs and claws are better developed than other parts of its body which allows it to make this journey.

When it arrives in the pouch, it weighs a gram or less, is about the size of a jelly bean, has no hair and is blind. It feeds on milk from its mother and as it grows stronger it begins to leave the pouch from time to time. The pouch may remain its home for up to a year.

TEXT C

Stars don't live forever but they do live for a very long time. Sometimes they last for billions of years. Stars are grouped together in galaxies. Our solar system is part of the Milky Way galaxy.

Stars begin to form when clouds of gas and dust join together in clumps. As these clumps expand, their gravity increases and more gas and dust are attracted to them. Eventually they begin to rotate and form into discs. As the discs expand further over time, they become a hot, solid core.

The core grows hotter as more and more gas and dust are pulled into it. During this process, hydrogen atoms fuse together and become atoms of helium gas. This creates energy that sets off a nuclear reaction and causes the star to shine. It takes about a million years from the time the gas cloud begins to collapse until the star that shines in our skies is created and a star is born.

TEXT D

21/2/2022: Yesterday I became a grandmother! Billy, our first grandson, was born at St George's hospital, Kew. The nine months since we first heard the news a baby was on its way went in a flash. Jess is well recovered from the birth, thank goodness. Gran will be so delighted. Billy is her first great-grandson.

In my view Billy has a strong family resemblance to our side of the family but Jim's parents say he has a strong family resemblance to their side! Time will tell. He is such a beautiful baby and I can't wait to spend time with him. Gran is in Tassie at the moment but will be back in two weeks. I told her yesterday that Billy will probably be talking and running around by then. ☺

But here's the amazing thing. Billy was born on 20 February at 2.20 pm; that is, at 2.20 on 20/2/2022. There is going to be a story about the chances of his being born at this moment in the local paper next week. I think I'll frame it, dear diary, to show Billy when he grows up.

Read the text below then answer the questions.

Maggie cuts her hair

'Go and speak to your aunts and uncles, my dears,' said Mrs Tulliver, looking anxious and melancholy. She wanted to whisper to Maggie a command to go and have her hair brushed.

'Well, and how do you do? And I hope you're good children, are you?' said Aunt Glegg, in the same loud, emphatic way, as she took their hands, hurting them with her large rings, and kissing their cheeks much against their desire. 'Look up, Tom, look up. Boys as go to boarding-schools should hold their heads up. Look at me now.' Tom declined that pleasure apparently, for he tried to draw his hand away. 'Put your hair behind your ears, Maggie, and keep your frock on your shoulder.'

[...]

'Well, my dears,' said aunt Pullet, in a compassionate voice, 'you grow wonderful fast. I doubt they'll outgrow their strength,' she added, looking over their heads, with a melancholy expression, at their mother. 'I think the gell has too much hair. I'd have it thinned and cut shorter, sister, if I was you; it isn't good for her health.

[...]

A dreadful resolve was gathering in Maggie's breast.

[...]

'Tom come out with me,' whispered Maggie, pulling his sleeve as she passed him; and Tom followed willingly enough.

'Come upstairs with me, Tom,' she whispered, when they were outside the door. 'There's something I want to do before dinner.'

'There's no time to play at anything before dinner,' said Tom, whose imagination was impatient of any intermediate prospect.

'Oh yes, there is time for this; *do* come, Tom.'

Tom followed Maggie upstairs into her mother's room, and saw her go at once to a drawer, from which she took out a large pair of scissors.

'What are they for, Maggie?' said Tom, feeling his curiosity awakened.

Maggie answered by seizing her front locks and cutting them straight across the middle of her forehead.

'Oh, my buttons! Maggie, you'll catch it!' exclaimed Tom; 'you'd better not cut any more off.'

Snip! went the great scissors again while Tom was speaking, and he couldn't help feeling it was rather good fun; Maggie would look so queer.

'Here, Tom, cut it behind for me,' said Maggie, excited by her own daring, and anxious to finish the deed.

'You'll catch it, you know,' said Tom, nodding his head in an admonitory manner, and hesitating a little as he took the scissors.

'Never mind, make haste!' said Maggie, giving a little stamp with her foot. Her cheeks were quite flushed.

The black locks were so thick, nothing could be more tempting to a lad who had already tasted the forbidden pleasure of cutting the pony's mane. I speak to those who know the satisfaction of making a pair of scissors meet through a duly resisting mass of hair. One delicious grinding snip, and then another and another, and the hinder-locks fell heavily on the floor, and Maggie stood cropped in a jagged, uneven manner, but with a sense of clearness and freedom, as if she had emerged from a wood into the open plain.

SAMPLE TEST 5

[...]

Maggie felt an unexpected pang. She had thought beforehand chiefly at her own deliverance from her teasing hair and teasing remarks about it, and something also of the triumph she should have over her mother and her aunts by this very decided course of action; she didn't want her hair to look pretty, - that was out of the question, - she only wanted people to think her a clever little girl, and not to find fault with her.

[...]

'Oh, Maggie, you'll have to go down to dinner directly,' said Tom. 'Oh, my!'

'Don't laugh at me, Tom,' said Maggie, in a passionate tone, with an outburst of angry tears, stamping, and giving him a push.

'Now, then, spitfire!' said Tom. 'What did you cut it off for, then? I shall go down: I can smell the dinner going in.'

He hurried downstairs and left poor Maggie to that bitter sense of the irrevocable which was almost an everyday experience of her small soul. She could see clearly enough, now the thing was done, that it was very foolish, and that she should have to hear and think more about her hair than ever.

From *The Mill on the Floss* by George Eliot

For questions **1–6**, choose the answer (**A, B, C** or **D**) which you think best answers the question.

1 Mrs Tulliver wants to 'whisper' to Maggie that she should get her hair brushed because

   A her voice is hoarse and she doesn't want to overuse it.

   B she doesn't want Tom to hear what she says to his sister.

   C she doesn't want Maggie's aunts to hear.

   D she is ashamed of how Maggie looks.

2 Maggie's aunts are presented by the author in a _____ light.

   A highly critical

   B warmly sympathetic

   C non-judgemental

   D faintly disapproving

3 Immediately after Tom finishes cutting her hair, Maggie feels

   A despairing.

   B set free.

   C triumphant.

   D horrified.

4 When she thinks more about the consequences of cutting her hair, Maggie feels

   A despairing.

   B set free.

   C triumphant.

   D horrified.

5 Tom's description of Maggie as a 'spitfire' is

   A unfair.

   B not at all justified.

   C unreasonable.

   D fairly accurate.

6 The main effect of the final paragraph is to

   A increase sympathy for Maggie's plight.

   B stress how foolish Maggie has been.

   C show Tom in a bad light.

   D reveal Maggie's ingratitude to her family.

Read the poem below by Zara Weil then answer the questions.

Hide and Seek

I decided to play a game with quiet
hide and seek
my turn
I slipped into the woods
looking for quiet
instead
a cacophony of forest-crackle
a hullabaloo of beast-babel
sprang towards me while
a tweedledum of pandemonium
circled above
it was a free-for-all
and even the sun
jangled copper
between the leaves
so much for the forest
I went to the sea
searching for quiet
but the waves trumpeted
a rumbling ruckus
a crash of crinkle-crests while
squarking gulls sky-dived into
wind-trembled sea and
tiny sea things zig-zagged
underfoot as a medley of
fat green seaweed
slapped the sand
non-stop non-stop
so much for the sea
but then I turned
and quiet tagged me
I stopped
forest stopped
sea stopped
I found quiet
it must have been hiding
the whole time
inside my words
inside of me

© Zara Weil; reproduced with permission

For questions 7–11, choose the answer (**A, B, C** or **D**) which you think best answers the question.

7   The speaker is playing a game of hide and seek with

A   her friends.

B   the forest.

C   the sea.

D   quiet.

8   The word 'cacophony' has been chosen especially for its _____ sounds.

A   harsh

B   melodious

C   gentle

D   spooky

9   What is the tone of the speaker's words 'so much for the forest'?

A   disappointment

B   anxiety

C   fury

D   bewilderment

10   The repetition of 'non-stop' echoes

A   the 'squarking' made by the birds.

B   the rhythm of the incessant beat of the waves.

C   the zig-zagging of the tiny sea things.

D   the trumpeting of the sea.

11   How does the speaker find quiet?

A   She looks for it.

B   She takes the first turn.

C   She stays well hidden.

D   It tags her.

Read the text below then answer the questions.

Six sentences have been removed from the text. Choose from the sentences (**A–G**) the one which fits each gap (**12–17**). There is one extra sentence which you do not need to use.

UFOs

UFOs are unidentified flying objects. They are aerial phenomena and cannot be immediately identified or explained. There is no question as to whether or not UFOs exist—they do exist. **12** _____ Those sightings that remain unexplained may well be caused by celestial, weather or planet phenomena. Or they could be the result of military exercises.

There is no real proof that any of the unidentified flying objects that have been sighted are of extraterrestrial origin. **13** _____ There is no evidence that UFOs are piloted by little green aliens or similar beings!

Governments take sightings of UFOs quite seriously. **14** _____ Many turn out to be fake but many sightings remain that have not been explained. Most people assume we don't yet have explanations for these unusual sightings. Others are convinced they house visitors who are aliens.

Could there be universes we know nothing about? **15** _____ It is possible, they claim, there could be planets inhabited by civilisations more advanced than our own.

There are numerous documented sightings still not fully understood. A wave of UFO sightings was reported in Belgium. **16** _____ The numbers claiming to see this UFO peaked on a night in late March, 1990. Three separate groups of police officers and around 13 500 people on the ground confirmed seeing a flat triangular shape with lights underneath.

Another example was the sighting at O'Hare airport in Chicago in November 2006. Twelve airport employees saw a metallic, saucer-shaped object hovering over Gate C-17. A more personal claim is of an attempted abduction by aliens in 1961 in New Hampshire. **17** _____ The details of their encounter are well documented and have baffled investigators to this day.

A	That is, that they come from outside the earth's atmosphere.
B	People regularly see objects flying in the atmosphere that are unable to be identified.
C	Some scientists claim it is clear that earth is not the only inhabited planet.
D	They keep careful records of sightings on file.
E	2022 could be a turning point in the study of UFOs.
F	These sightings lasted from 1989 to 1990.
G	It was reported by an American couple, Barney and Betty Hill.

SAMPLE TEST 5

Read the four texts below on the theme of survival.

For questions **18–25**, choose the option (**A, B, C** or **D**) which you think best answers the question.

Which text ...

18 refs to a hostile event that left few survivors? _____

19 mentions two different types of animal who survive well in a similar environment? _____

20 explains how a group of children survived an accident? _____

21 gives details of an individual's approach to survival? _____

22 demonstrates how human beings and the natural world can help each other survive? _____

23 lists hardships to be overcome in order to survive? _____

24 refers to something that has adapted to surviving in any environment? _____

25 describes how a particular culture views survival skills? _____

TEXT A

September 30, 1659. I, poor miserable Robinson Crusoe, being shipwrecked during a dreadful storm in the offing, came on shore on this dismal, unfortunate island, which I called 'The Island of Despair'; all the rest of the ship's company being drowned, and myself almost dead.

All the rest of the day I spent in afflicting myself at the dismal circumstances I was brought to—viz. I had neither food, house, clothes, weapon, nor place to fly to; and in despair of any relief, saw nothing but death before me—either that I should be devoured by wild beasts, murdered by savages, or starved to death for want of food.

[...]

From the 1st of October to the 24th. All these days entirely spent in many several voyages to get all I could out of the ship, which I brought on shore every tide of flood upon rafts.

[...]

Nov. 4. The working part of this day and of the next were wholly employed in making my table, for I was yet but a very sorry workman, though time and necessity made me a complete natural mechanic soon after, as I believe they would do anyone else.

From *The Life and Adventures of Robinson Crusoe* by Daniel Defoe

TEXT B

On September 11, 2001 terrorist highjackers flew into the Twin Towers of New York's World Trade Centre and destroyed them. Around 3000 people, including many firefighters, were killed and about 6000 injured. Rescuers found only 20 or so survivors in the wreckage in the weeks that followed.

The last living thing removed from the site was the Callery Pear tree, dubbed the Survivor Tree. The tree had grown between the Twin Towers. It was badly damaged as its roots and branches were broken and burned. It was cared for at a nursery in the Bronx. While there, it survived further 'attacks'—a fence falling on it and a hurricane. In 2010 it was returned and replanted at the foot of the towers besides many other trees planted as a Memorial for a disaster that shook the world. Today, its new limbs can be seen growing vigorously from its gnarled stumps. Each year seeds taken from the tree are sent to communities affected by tragedies.

TEXT C

Animals need skills to survive, especially in the wild. These skills include, for example, being strong and powerful enough to protect their territory and their young; using camouflage, speed or other skills to evade predators; and being able to threaten and overcome prey with ease.

A further skill that can help the survival of an animal species is the ability to adapt well to difficult or changing environments. Camels, for example, can go without water for long periods of time. They can sweat about a quarter of their water content without becoming dehydrated. This makes them very suited to life in the desert. Camel spiders (no relation!) are vicious predators. They are fast runners and can run up to 16 kilometres per hour. They are also well adapted to desert living.

Cockroaches are very difficult to get rid of as they move swiftly, hide well in nooks and crevices, and are resistant to all types of deadly sprays and poisons. They have proved able to adapt to living almost anywhere. Some people believe they'll be the only survivors at the end of the world.

TEXT D

Torres Strait Islander culture involves elders teaching survival skills to their children from a very early age. Children grow up knowing, for example, what they can safely eat and drink on an island, how the tides operate and how to navigate. They learn to swim and fish and to avoid danger by staying together.

In 2004 three young children—Ellis, Norita and Bala—put what they had learned into practice. They were travelling with their parents and little brother to Thursday Island, for a twenty-first birthday celebration. The family was crowded into a 5-metre dinghy and conditions became rough and windy. When the motor broke down, and the seas grew wilder, their dinghy sank. Their parents told the three older children to swim to the nearest island.

About four hours later they were washed up on a rocky outcrop. Their only food was oysters and after four days there they swam through treacherous waters to an island six kilometres away. This time they found coconuts and berries. They planned to island-hop home but miraculously their uncle found them. Sadly their parents and brother were not found.

SAMPLE TEST 6

Read the text below then answer the questions.

Lost in the woods

The next morning, we can hear the soft thud of cannon fire again, but the snow is still falling steadily so we stay. Besides, where would we go? We don't even know where we are, or what lies beyond the farmyard and the ring of forest that surrounds us.

Otto presses his face against the window and stares at the barn. 'It looks like a gingerbread house with thick icing all over the roof.'

'Like in *Hansel and Gretel*,' I suggest.

'Yes!' He turns to me, his face alight as he recalls the fairy tale.

Otto is so easily lost in the moment. Dying of a broken heart. Seething, bubbling, boiling with anger. Gobbling his favourite foods. Beaming with happiness.

I join him at the window, my shoulder pressed against his, and peer out at the gingerbread barn and the sugar frosted forest beyond. It is a fairy-tale land that has been kept safe from the war that rages all around. But then I shudder and turn away, because even the most beautiful fairy-tale land has a wicked witch lurking somewhere nearby.

Mia waddles toward us, her golden hair standing on end. She scrunches her nose.

'Mia wet.'

'Mia smelly!,' cries Otto.

'Mia bath!' I shout.

We find a tub and drag it in front of the fire. It takes an hour to boil the water and fill the tub. But it's worth it. Otto's and Mia's faces grin up at me through the soap suds.

[...]

The photographs that were stuffed down our underwear sit on the mantelpiece. Mama, Papa, Oma and Opa smile down at me from one photo. Mama, Papa, Otto, Mia and Liesl smile down at me from the other. I start reciting the family tree– first, middle, last names of everyone in the Wolf family – just as Opa made me on that last morning we were together.

Otto appears in the doorway from the bedroom. He's wearing a man's undershirt that reaches to his ankles and a pale blue lady's hat with a bow on one side.

'I've found some clothes!' he cries. 'Lots of soft, clean clothes to keep us warm. Even children's clothes. They're all for boys but you can pretend to be a boy.' He grins. 'I always wanted a big brother.'

I throw the cake of soap at him from the bath.

****

SAMPLE TEST 6

There is everything we need in the chest of drawers. The boys' clothes are just the right size for Otto and me.

'I like the feel of long-johns and trousers,' I tell Otto.

'They're so much warmer than a skirt and tights.'

'I like this hat,' says Otto, putting the pretty blue hat back on his head once he's fully dressed.

I pull a jumper over Mia's head and roll up the sleeves to let her hands poke free. I tie a knitted bonnet beneath her chin, kiss her cheek, and sing 'Clean, warm clothes!'

'Stolen clothes!' shouts Otto. Tilting the pretty blue hat at a jaunty angle.

'Not stolen,' I say. 'Borrowed.'

Otto scrunches his nose. 'So we'll give them back?'

I look down at the red jumper I'm wearing. It's thick and warm and so much cleaner than the one I peeled off before my bath.

I blush. 'No we won't give them back.'

'So we *are* stealing,' says Otto. 'We're thieves. Again!'

'I bite my lip.

'Just until the war is over,' I explain.

'How long will that be?' he asks.

'Soon. And when we get back home, we can buy some new clothes for the people that live here. We'll send them a parcel. It will be a kind of thank-you gift for letting us stay and for using all their things.'

Otto grins. He likes the idea.

I like the idea too, but I can't help feeling as if I've just told a terrible lie. A bundle of terrible lies.

I am a burglar, a thief, a vandal *and* a liar.

From *We are Wolves* by Katrina Nannestad
© Katrina Nannestad; reproduced with permission

For questions **1–6**, choose the answer (**A, B, C** or **D**) which you think best answers the question.

1 Where are the children?

A living by themselves in a farmhouse

B hiding in a farmhouse while a war is going on

C playing in a gingerbread house

D living with Oma and Opa while their parents are away

2 The narrator of the story is

A the author.

B Otto Wolf.

C Otto Wolf's older sister.

D Otto Wolf's big brother.

3 The children are extremely dirty because

A they don't like taking baths.

B it is too cold to wash.

C their parents are neglecting them.

D they haven't had a place to wash until now.

4 What kind of person is Otto?

A intense

B coolheaded

C sensible

D heartless

5 The narrator blushes when Otto asks if they'll give back the clothes because

A she thinks he wants to steal them.

B she feels guilty.

C she is embarrassed she has chosen a thick, warm jumper for herself.

D she has let Otto have fun with dressing up in the clothes.

6 In the last line, the narrator judges herself

A much too harshly.

B fairly.

C not harshly enough.

D predictably.

Read the poem below by Dorothea Mackellar then answer the questions.

My Country

The love of field and coppice,
Of green and shaded lanes,
Of ordered woods and gardens
Is running in your veins;
Strong love of grey-blue distance,
Brown streams and soft, dim skies—
I know but cannot share it,
My love is otherwise.

I love a sunburnt country,
A land of sweeping plains,
Of ragged mountain ranges,
Of droughts and flooding rains;
I love her far horizons,
I love her jewel-sea,
Her beauty and her terror—
The wide brown land for me!

[...]

Core of my heart, my country!
Her pitiless blue sky,
When sick at heart, around us
We see the cattle die—
But then the grey clouds gather
And we can bless again
The drumming of an army,
The steady, soaking rain.

[...]

An opal-hearted country,
A wilful, lavish land—
All you who have not loved her,
You will not understand—
Though earth holds many splendours,
Wherever I may die,
I know to what brown country
My homing thoughts will fly.

For questions 7–11, choose the answer (**A, B, C** or **D**) which you think best answers the question.

7 Stanza one mainly describes a world of
  A disarray.
  B soft colours.
  C orderliness.
  D shadow.

8 Stanza two mainly describes a world of
  A contrasts.
  B suffering.
  C beauty.
  D space.

9 The word 'sunburnt' is used to suggest a country where
  A people visit the beach.
  B summers are fierce.
  C climate change has taken its toll.
  D the land is on fire.

10 The speaker sees the 'terror' of her country as something to be
  A accepted.
  B rejected.
  C ignored.
  D embraced.

11 The poet's feelings for her country are best described as
  A warmly affectionate.
  B fairly supportive.
  C wildly passionate.
  D quite patriotic.

SAMPLE TEST 6

Read the text below then answer the questions.

Six sentences have been removed from the text. Choose from the sentences (**A–G**) the one which fits each gap (**12–17**). There is one extra sentence which you do not need to use.

Kites

Kites usually have a light frame covered with thin material such as paper, nylon or silk. **12** _____ It has a long string attached to the frame which allows the kite to be flown in the wind. There are many variations in the appearance and size of kites, ranging from simple designs to magnificent works of art.

Kites have a long history. **13** _____ Chinese, Japanese and Indian cultures, for example, have records of stories, illustrations and artefacts of kites in their ancient histories. Marco Polo, a merchant from Venice who visited China, is credited with introducing the idea of the kite to Europe. **14** _____ When he returned home to Italy, he passed on stories about the kites he had seen and the strange purposes for which he saw them used.

Different cultures are often famous for particular ways they have made use of kites. **15** _____ There are legends of a small Chinese General in 200 BC who was flown over the emperor's palace in a kite at night and the enemy soldiers fled thinking he was a ghost! Malay fishermen attach them to their boats as lures that skim the water with live baits to catch surface-feeding predators. In Bali, kites are flown during the dry season to give thanks for a profitable harvest.

Many uses for kites cross cultural boundaries. They have proved particularly useful in scientific experiments in many different countries. **16** _____ Collecting weather data is another scientific way kites have been used, although newer methods have helped to bring an end to this practice.

Other ways kites are commonly used across cultures include in agriculture as scarecrows to frighten birds from eating crops. **17** _____ Most famously, young children love to fly their kites in their local park, all over the world.

A	He journeyed there on the Silk Road, a trade route joining East and West, towards the end of the 13th century.
B	Chinese armies, for example, have used them as instruments of warfare in strategies to defeat their enemies.
C	The earliest known examples are from Asia from some two and three thousand years ago.
D	They provide entertainment for audiences of young and old at kite festivals to celebrate cultural or spiritual events.
E	Kite fights have been banned in some countries.
F	Measuring distances, calculating wind readings and assisting with experiments related to flight are examples.
G	The frame often has a tail to stabilise it.

Read the four texts below on the theme of marine animals.

For questions **18–25**, choose the option (**A, B, C** or **D**) which you think best answers the question.

Which text ...

18 includes a talking marine creature? _____

19 refers to artificially made marine mammals? _____

20 mentions an indigenous attitude to a particular marine animal? _____

21 describes a feature that is like a human thumbprint? _____

22 suggests people are more ecologically aware now than previously? _____

23 is about the role of one of the five senses in the life of marine animals? _____

24 does not include an animal character with a human name? _____

25 tells the story of a scientific error? _____

TEXT A

The film *Jaws* began life as a novel by Peter Benchley and came to the screen in 1974. Steven Spielberg directed the film. The plot is simple. A young woman is killed by a great white shark when swimming off an island near a popular tourist town. Police want to close the beaches but the mayor won't allow it, fearing his town won't survive the loss of tourist revenue. It is decided that instead they must capture the shark.

Jaws was filmed on location at Martha's Vineyard in Massachusetts. You can imagine the problems that arose: how to make the violent attack on the girl look real (they used underwater cables to drag her around); how to get a big enough shark to film as the 'maneater' transported to the location in good condition; and how to make their mechanical sharks, all nicknamed Bruce, function correctly (they had to build three different versions of their 1.2-ton predator).

Today people have a much better understanding of the important role sharks play in the ecosystem and would strongly protest at the idea of a shark being killed—even if only in a movie.

TEXT B

When dinosaurs, such as the Stegosaurus and the Tyrannosaurus rex, roamed the earth around 380 million years ago, lungfish swam in the rivers nearby. Since lungfish have both lungs and gills, scientists view them as the link between fish and amphibians.

Those who take care of lungfish in aquariums claim they have individual personalities. Methuselah, who is thought to be at least 90 years old, lives in an aquarium in Chicago. Methuselah, like all lungfish, is omnivorous. She is well known for her gourmet tastes: prawns in winter, smelt in springtime and figs for a treat. She is probably the oldest fish living in an aquarium in the world right now.

Early settlers in Australia caught and ate lungfish. The Gubbi Gubbi people of Queensland think of them as sacred and do not eat or kill them.

TEXT C

Scientists have been researching clams for centuries. I am a clam. My name is Ming the Mollusc. I should say I *was* a clam, past tense. Now I am a ghost. Life as a ghost is quite pleasant. I can wander undisturbed through my much-loved home, the sea. But I think it is important my family know how I came to die.

Clams have a reputation for living very long lives. Scientists have worked out a way to find out our ages by counting the annual growth bands on a particular part of our shells. Scientists are interested in us because they want to know more about why we live so long.

That's all very well but when scientists dredged me up from off the coast of Iceland in 2006 to begin their research, they accidently killed me. They cut my 507 years of life short! I forgave them as they were very sorry and at least I'm in the *Guinness Book of Records* now.

TEXT D

Sound is very important to marine animals as it lets them gather information about their surroundings and communicate across distances. They rely on sound to locate food and it plays an important part in marine mammal survival.

Fish, for example, make sounds such as grunts, clicks and snaps to attract mates and ward off predators. Dolphins communicate with each other mainly through squeaks, clicks and whistles. Bottlenose dolphins use individual whistles that are like a signature or identifying feature. Mothers whistle continuously to their babies who recognise the unique pattern of their sounds.

Some whales, such as the toothed whale, also use high-frequency clicks and whistles to communicate. Male humpbacks, minkes and some blue and fin whales are famous for their melodious songs. They have vocal cords in their voice boxes as we do, although they use them differently so they don't run out of breath by losing air!

Read the text below then answer the questions.

How the camel got his hump

In the beginning of years, when the world was so new and all, and the Animals were just beginning to work for Man, there was a Camel, and he lived in the middle of a Howling Desert because he did not want to work; and besides, he was a Howler himself. So he ate sticks and thorns and tamarisks and milkweed and prickles, most excruciating idle; and when anybody spoke to him he said 'Humph!' Just 'Humph!' and no more.

Presently the Horse came to him on Monday morning, with a saddle on his back and a bit in his mouth, and said, 'Camel, O Camel, come out and trot like the rest of us.'

'Humph!' said the Camel; and the Horse went away and told the Man.

Presently the Dog came to him, with a stick in his mouth, and said, 'Camel, O Camel, come and fetch and carry like the rest of us.'

'Humph!' said the Camel; and the Dog went away and told the Man.

Presently the Ox came to him, with the yoke on his neck and said, 'Camel, O Camel, come and plough like the rest of us.'

'Humph!' said the Camel; and the Ox went away and told the Man.

At the end of the day the Man called the Horse and the Dog and the Ox together, and said, 'Three, O Three, I'm very sorry for you (with the world so new-and-all); but that Humph-thing in the Desert can't work, or he would have been here by now, so I am going to leave him alone, and you must work double-time to make up for it.'

That made the Three very angry (with the world so new-and-all), and they held a palaver, and an *indaba*, and a *punchayet*, and a pow-wow on the edge of the Desert; and the Camel came chewing on milkweed *most* excruciating idle, and laughed at them. Then he said 'Humph!' and went away again.

Presently there came along the Djinn in charge of All Deserts, rolling in a cloud of dust (Djinns always travel that way because it is Magic), and he stopped to palaver and pow-pow with the Three.

'Djinn of All Deserts,' said the Horse, 'is it right for anyone to be idle, with the world so new-and-all?'

'Certainly not,' said the Djinn.

'Well,' said the Horse, 'there's a thing in the middle of your Howling Desert (and he's a Howler himself) with a long neck and long legs, and he hasn't done a stroke of work since Monday morning. He won't trot.'

'Whew!' said the Djinn, whistling, 'that's my Camel, for all the gold in Arabia! What does he say about it?'

'He says 'Humph!'' said the Dog; 'and he won't fetch and carry.'

'Does he say anything else?'

'Only 'Humph!'; and he won't plough,' said the Ox.

'Very good,' said the Djinn. 'I'll humph him if you will kindly wait a minute.'

The Djinn rolled himself up in his dust-cloak, and took a bearing across the desert, and found the Camel most excruciatingly idle, looking at his own reflection in a pool of water.

'My long and bubbling friend,' said the Djinn, 'what's this I hear of your doing no work, with the world so new-and-all?'

'Humph!' said the Camel.

The Djinn sat down, with his chin in his hand, and began to think a Great Magic, while the Camel looked at his own reflection in the pool of water.

'You've given the Three extra work ever since Monday morning, all on account of your excruciating idleness,' said the Djinn; and he went on thinking Magics, with his chin in his hand.

'Humph!' said the Camel.

'I shouldn't say that again if I were you,' said the Djinn; you might say it once too often. Bubbles, I want you to work.'

And the Camel said 'Humph!' again; but no sooner had he said it than he saw his back, that he was so proud of, puffing up and puffing up into a great big lolloping humph.

'Do you see that?' said the Djinn. 'That's your very own humph that you've brought upon your very own self by not working. To-day is Thursday, and you've done no work since Monday, when the work began. Now you are going to work.'

'How can I,' said the Camel, 'with this humph on my back?'

'That's made a-purpose,' said the Djinn, 'all because you missed those three days. You will be able to work now for three days without eating, because you can live on your humph; and don't you ever say I never did anything for you. Come out of the Desert and go to the Three, and behave. Humph yourself!'

And the Camel humphed himself, humph and all, and went away to join the Three. And from that day to this the Camel always wears a humph (we call it 'hump' now, not to hurt his feelings); but he has never yet caught up with the three days that he missed at the beginning of the world, and he has never yet learned how to behave.

From 'How the camel got his hump' from *Just So Stories* by Rudyard Kipling

SAMPLE TEST 7

For questions **1–6**, choose the answer (**A, B, C** or **D**) which you think best answers the question.

1 When does this story take place?

A outside time

B near the beginning of the world

C near the end of the world

D before time began

2 The Camel's most irritating characteristic is its

A vanity.

B rudeness.

C laziness.

D dishonesty.

3 How does the Camel's behaviour affect the other animals?

A It makes the Man cross with them.

B They begin to copy the Camel.

C They decide to summon the Djinn.

D They have to do the Camel's share of work.

4 The Djinn makes the camel say 'Humph' by

A talking to it rudely.

B using his magic.

C tricking it to say what he wants it to say.

D laughing at its behaviour.

5 The Djinn's plan is

A ingenious.

B problematic.

C unimaginative.

D impractical.

6 How is the Camel changed by the Djinn?

A It becomes a willing worker.

B It learns to respect the other animals.

C It becomes much more disobedient.

D It gains a hump and starts working.

Read the poem by TS Eliot then answer the questions.

Macavity: The Mystery Cat

Macavity's a Mystery Cat: he's called the
   Hidden Paw—
For he's the master criminal who can defy the
   Law.
He's the bafflement of Scotland Yard, the Flying
   Squad's despair:
For when they reach the scene of crime—
   Macavity's not there!

[...]

Macavity's a ginger cat, he's very tall and thin;
You would know him if you saw him, for his eyes
   are sunken in.
His brow is deeply lined with thought, his head is
   highly domed;
His coat is dusty from neglect, his whiskers are
   uncombed.
He sways his head from side to side, with
   movements like a snake;
And when you think he's half asleep, he's always
   wide awake.

[...]

He's outwardly respectable. (They say he cheats
   at cards.)
And his footprints are not found in any file of
   Scotland Yard's.
And when the larder's looted, or the jewel-case
   is rifled,
Or when the milk is missing, or another Peke's
   been stifled,
Or the greenhouse glass is broken, and the trellis
   past repair—
Ay, there's the wonder of the thing! *Macavity's
   not there*!

And when the Foreign Office find a Treaty's
   gone astray,
Or the Admiralty lose some plans and drawings
   by the way,
There may be a scrap of paper in the hall or on
   the stair—
But it's useless to investigate—*Macavity's not
   there*!
And when the loss has been disclosed, the
   Secret Service say:
'It *must* have been Macavity!'—but he's a mile
   away.
You'll be sure to find him resting, or a-licking of
   his thumbs,
Or engaged in doing complicated long division
   sums.

Macavity, Macavity, there's no one like Macavity,
There never was a Cat of such deceitfulness and
   suavity.
He always has an alibi, and one or two to spare:
At whatever time the deed took place—
   MACAVITY WASN'T THERE!
And they say that all the Cats whose wicked
   deeds are widely known
(I might mention Mungojerrie, I might mention
   Griddlebone)
Are nothing more than agents for the Cat who
   all the time
Just controls their operations: the Napoleon* of
   Crime!

* Napoleon was a famous French military and political
   leader.

From *Old Possum's Book of Practical Cats* by TS Eliot

For questions **7–11**, choose the answer (**A, B, C** or **D**) which you think best answers the question.

7 Macavity is called a 'Mystery Cat' mainly because he

A likes to break the law.

B is a criminal.

C is expert at disappearing.

D pretends he's asleep when he's awake.

8 The word 'looted' suggests Macavity's behaviour is

A frightening.

B reasonable.

C criminal.

D naughty.

9 Macavity's crimes are

_____ by the poet.

A made to seem trivial

B exaggerated and dramatised

C played down in importance

D given a fair, accurate account

10 The poet's attitude to Macavity is mainly

A hatred.

B dislike.

C awe.

D disgust.

11 How does Macavity manage to always have 'an alibi'?

A He can change his shape if he needs to disappear.

B No-one knows how he does this.

C He keeps his whereabouts secret.

D He controls an 'army' of cats who obey his orders.

Read the text below then answer the questions.

Six sentences have been removed from the text. Choose from the sentences (**A–G**) the one which fits each gap (**12–17**). There is one extra sentence which you do not need to use.

Men's hairstyles

Why do men wear their hair in different styles in different periods of time? **12** _____ It can also be to make a statement of some kind, to support a belief or for some more practical reason.

Paintings from the Bronze and Iron ages (1200–500 BC) depict people from the Eastern Mediterranean, North Africa and the Near East with braided hair. Braiding the hair in China was encouraged by Confucian beliefs. **13** _____ During the Qing dynasty in China (1636–1912), for example, men were required to wear their hair shaved off at the front of the head with the rest of their hair tied or braided.

In Europe in the Middle Ages, there was a period of time when the bowl cut for men became very common. **14** _____ In fact, that was often exactly the way the cut was carried out! What about wigs? The popularity of large, powdered wigs for men peaked in the 18th century in Europe. When a heavy tax to help fund the Napoleonic wars was introduced on hair powder towards the end of the century, wigs fell out of favour.

Men's hairstyles are sometimes influenced by military needs. **15** _____ They shaved the top of their heads and pulled the rest of their hair into a topknot. This practice has come and gone over time but Sumo wrestlers still favour a version of the topknot, or a 'man-bun' as it has more recently been called. In contrast many modern armies favour short hair. **16** _____ Induction cuts, the shortest possible haircut without using a razor, are given to new recruits in the armed forces in the United States, for example.

In modern times in Australia, you are likely to see men with a variety of hairstyles. **17** _____ You'll also see short back and sides, ponytails, loose hanging locks and everything in between—even the occasional mullet.

A	This style looked as if a bowl had been placed on the head and then scissors had been used to cut around its shape.
B	It is often related to following a fashion that is in vogue.
C	From as long ago as the ninth century, Samurai warriors have had their hair cut in a style designed to stabilise their helmets during battle.
D	If you visit your local mall, you'll see men with part shaving and undercutting styles.
E	This is because short hair is easily managed and easy to keep clean and well groomed.
F	The cutting of hair was frowned on as it was viewed as a gift from ancestors.
G	A mullet has long hair at the back with trimmed sides and top.

SAMPLE TEST 7

Read the four texts below on the theme of journeys.

For questions **18–25**, choose the option (**A, B, C** or **D**) which you think best answers the question.

Which text ...

18 includes information related to a species that would be of concern to conservationists? _____

19 implies the journeys described are inspired by a longing to be home? _____

20 mentions using the internet for communication purposes? _____

21 reveals the way a series of journeys can better a human community? _____

22 is about a journey inspired by listening to a book? _____

23 does not include any reference to books? _____

24 refers to the emotional impact a single journey can bring about? _____

25 is about a special kind of co-operation between human and animal? _____

TEXT A

Birds generally migrate because food or good nesting locations become scarce. They fly to another place where the resources they need are in better supply. When these become depleted, they return to their original location. Some birds travel extraordinary distances in the process.

The Arctic Tern, for example, migrates from the north to the south pole—a round trip of between 30 000 and 40 000 kilometres. The Short-tailed Shearwater, an Australian seabird, leaves its young chicks behind and flies from Australia to the southern winter in Japan, Siberia and Alaska. The Bar-tailed Godwit does something even more extraordinary. On its flight from Alaska in the north to Australia and New Zealand in the south, it flies about 12 000 km, over seven or eight days and nights, without ever stopping!

When Bar-tailed Godwits make their return flight they need to stop and rest when they near the Yellow Sea wetlands in Asia. Suitable places for them to recuperate have been disappearing because of changes and developments made by humans to these areas—a cause for alarm as some have noted.

Arctic tern

TEXT B

Jessica Watson had an ambition. She wanted to sail around the world in a yacht, by herself, before her 17th birthday. She was inspired by a story her mother read to her: *Lionheart: A Journey of the Human Spirit*, a book by Jesse Martin who had successfully undertaken a similar journey.

Jessica left Sydney on *Ella's Pink Lady* on 18 October 2019. On her journey she kept a blog that became very popular. In one comment she claimed she could write about a fly landing on her yacht and someone would find that interesting. The 447 comments that followed this remark confirmed that belief. Her blog proved a great way for her to connect with people and find encouragement as she battled alone through huge seas or across long stretches of boredom.

The journey lasted 210 days. On May 15, 2010 Jessica arrived in Sydney having completed her circumnavigation single-handed, without stopping and with three days to go until she turned 17. Jessica made history as the youngest person to achieve such a feat. She was named young Australian of the year in 2011.

TEXT C

Luis Soriano lives in La Gloria, a small town in rural Colombia. Its people struggle with poverty. As a primary teacher Luis knows how difficult it is for children, especially in the remoter areas, to have access to books to read. Luis felt he had to find a way to bring books to these children. His idea was to use his donkeys to carry him and a library of books to wherever they lived. He made this idea a reality and in the late 1990s the Biblioburro, The Donkey Library, was born.

To begin with, Luis had around 70 books in his travelling library. Now he has gathered donations of hundreds of books and an actual library has been built next to his home to house them. He still sets off each weekend with his donkeys loaded with books, knowing he will face many dangers on the way (armed conflict and crime are not uncommon in these areas). A round trip takes him about eight hours. His reward is the pleasure the children show when he arrives and their delight in talking with him about the books he brings them.

TEXT D

There are many stories of animals making incredible journeys to find their way back to their home. Dogs are particularly famous for journeys of this kind. In her book *Incredible Dog Journeys*, Laura Greaves describes sixteen true stories about dogs who overcame extraordinary difficulties and travelled over vast distances to find their way back to their homes. One of these stories is about a Hungarian Vizsla named Penny. She was dognapped and taken over 6000 kilometres away. Yet she found her way back to her owner!

These stories make good reading and viewing. *The Incredible Journey*, for example, a novel by Sheila Burnford that was made into a film by Disney, is about the adventures of a Labrador Retriever, a Bull Terrier and a Siamese cat who travel 400 kilometres through the Canadian wilderness to get back to their home. *Lassie Come Home*, a novel by Eric Knight, also made into a film, tells how Lassie, a Border Collie, travels from Scotland back to her old home in Yorkshire. The scene where she is reunited with Jo, her much-loved young owner, is definitely a tear jerker!

SAMPLE TEST 8

Read the text below then answer the questions.

The Coral Island

It was a bright, beautiful, warm day when our ship spread her canvas to the breeze and sailed for the regions of the south. Oh, how my heart bounded with delight as I listened to the merry chorus of the sailors while they hauled at the ropes and got in the anchor! The captain shouted; the men ran to obey; the noble ship bent over to the breeze, and the shore gradually faded from my view; while I stood looking on, with a kind of feeling that the whole was a delightful dream.

The first thing that struck me as being different from anything I had yet seen during my short career on the sea, was the hoisting of the anchor on deck and lashing it firmly down with ropes, as if we had now bid adieu to the land for ever and would require its services no more.

'There, lass!' cried a broad-shouldered Jack Tar*, giving the fluke of the anchor a hearty slap with his hand after the housing was completed—'there, lass, take a good nap now, for we shan't ask you to kiss the mud again for many a long day to come!'

And so it was. That anchor did not 'kiss the mud' for many long days afterwards; and when at last it did, it was for the last time!

[...]

One night, soon after we entered the tropics, an awful storm burst upon our ship. The first squall of wind carried away two of our masts, and left only the foremast standing. Even this, however, was more than enough, for we did not dare to hoist a rag of sail on it. For five days the tempest raged in all its fury. Everything was swept off the decks, except one small boat. The steersman was lashed to the wheel lest he should be washed away, and we all gave ourselves up for lost. The captain said that he had no idea where we were, as we had been blown far out of our course; and we feared much that we might get among the dangerous coral reefs which are so numerous in the Pacific. At daybreak on the sixth morning of the gale we saw land ahead; it was an island encircled by a reef of coral, on which the waves broke in fury. There was calm water within this reef, but we could see only one narrow opening into it. For this opening we steered; but ere we reached it a tremendous wave broke on our stern, tore the rudder completely off, and left us at the mercy of the winds and waves.

'It's all over with us now, lads!' said the captain to the men. 'Get the boat ready to launch; we shall be on the rocks in less than half-an-hour.'

The men obeyed in gloomy silence, for they felt that there was little hope of so small a boat living in such a sea.

'Come, boys,' said Jack Martin, in a grave tone, to me and Peterkin, as we stood on the quarter-deck awaiting our fate—'come, boys; we three shall stick together. You see it is impossible that the little boat can reach the shore, crowded with men. It will be sure to upset, so I mean rather to trust myself to a large oar. I see through the telescope that the ship will strike at the tail of the reef, where the waves break into the quiet water inside; so if we manage to cling to the oar till it is driven over the breakers, we may perhaps gain the shore. What say you? Will you join me?'

We gladly agreed to follow Jack, for he inspired us with confidence—although I could perceive, by the sad tone of his voice, that he had little hope.

[...]

The ship was now very near the rocks. The men were ready with the boat, and the captain beside them giving orders, when a tremendous wave came towards us. We three ran towards the bow to lay hold of our oar, and had barely reached it when the wave fell on the deck with a crash like thunder. At the same moment the ship struck; the foremast broke off close to the deck and went over the side, carrying the boat and men along with it. Our oar got entangled with the wreck, and Jack seized an axe to cut it free; but owing to the motion of the ship, he missed the cordage and struck the axe deep into the oar. Another wave, however, washed it clear of the wreck. We all seized hold of it, and the next instant we were struggling in the wild sea. The last thing I saw was the boat whirling in the surf, and all the sailors tossed into the foaming waves. Then I became insensible.

On recovering from my swoon I found myself lying on a bank of soft grass, under shelter of an overhanging rock, with Peterkin on his knees by my side, tenderly bathing my temples with water, and endeavouring to stop the blood that flowed from a wound in my forehead.

*sailor

From *The Coral Island* by RM Ballantyne

For questions **1–6**, choose the answer (**A, B, C** or **D**) which you think best answers the question.

1 This text can best be described as being from

  A a science-fiction novel.

  B a fairytale.

  C an adventure story.

  D a fable.

2 The mood of the opening is
_____ that of the ending.

  A very similar to

  B more joyous than

  C more dramatic than

  D more dreamlike than

3 The 'lass' referred to is

  A the ship.

  B the Jack Tar's wife.

  C the anchor.

  D a sleepy girl on board.

4 Which event ensures the sailors are likely to be shipwrecked?

  A the rudder being torn off

  B the lashing of the steersman to the wheel

  C their being blown off course

  D the loss of the ship's masts

5 What contributed most to saving the narrator from drowning?

  A Peterkin's kindness

  B Jack's plan

  C the narrator's strength

  D the wildness of the sea

6 What is most likely to have been the fate of the rest of the sailors?

  A They escaped in their small boat.

  B They fell from the boat into the wild sea.

  C They escaped to a coral island.

  D They perished in the sea.

Read the poem below by Nairn Kennedy then answer the questions.

'This idea came from visiting a certain well-known coffee chain which asks you for your first name to identify which coffee is yours, and turned into an exploration of the alienation felt by an immigrant. Sometimes a poem takes over from the writer and develops its own theme, which is a reason why we write.'

The Lie

Once, I had a name as smooth and clear
as all the streams of Poland; it poured
    through ears
like melting snow; but over here
it warped to ugly consonants
which clattered off your tongues
like Scrabble tiles.
In the local coffee shop last week,
baristas pounded out their war drums,
bashing out the grit of coffee grounds.
What name? said the Recording Angel at the
    counter,
poised with a tattered ballpoint and plastic
    cup;
the queue behind me snorted in frustration.
I stared straight through my spectacles and
    hers
into brown eyes. *Jim*, I said, biting
a suddenly unwieldy tongue.

■ For questions **7–11**, choose the answer (**A, B, C** or **D**) which you think best answers the question.

7 His name 'poured through ears / like melting snow' implies

  A no-one commented on it.

  B it was a popular name.

  C it sounded smooth and mellifluous.

  D it was spelt correctly.

8 Once the narrator moves away from Poland

  A he forgets his Polish name.

  B he always calls himself Jim.

  C he wishes he was back there.

  D he feels embarrassed when his name is said aloud.

9 The narrator makes the atmosphere at the coffee shop seem

  A cheerful.

  B threatening.

  C uncomfortable.

  D relaxing.

10 What is the 'lie' of the title of the poem?

  A He doesn't know his name.

  B He says his name is Jim.

  C He bites his tongue.

  D His Polish name 'poured' through ears.

11 How does the narrator feel about his lie?

  A uneasy

  B proud

  C terrified

  D confident

Read the text below then answer the questions.

Six sentences have been removed from the text. Choose from the sentences (**A–G**) the one which fits each gap (**12–17**). There is one extra sentence which you do not need to use.

Pretzel's Story

Pretzel, a green turtle hatchling, was recently washed ashore by flood waters. **12** _____ Luckily the tiny turtle was rescued and, along with other rescue animals including echidnas, was taken to Byron Bay Wildlife Hospital.

The staff at the hospital recognised Pretzel had a further problem. **13** _____ He had eaten a piece of plastic that had lodged there. The vet gave him a laxative which helped him remove it from its body.

At Byron Bay, there were concerns about the seawater available for housing the turtle hatchling and other rescued sea creatures. **14** _____ As a result, the rescued sea creatures were transferred to Sea World on the Gold Coast. It was at Sea World that it was found Pretzel had even more plastic in his body. A marine scientist was alerted to this when she noticed two small pieces of plastic floating in his tank. Pretzel had got rid of these through his gut but was unable to get rid of another larger piece. **15** _____ Pretzel had now used up three of his lives!

As you can imagine, scientists are horrified by the damage caused by plastics and microplastics to marine life. **16** _____ Flooding has further escalated the plastic problem. Quantities of debris and plastics are flushed into the ocean, increasing pollution levels. This situation can only get worse according to environmentalists.

Mr James Weiss, a marine specialist who writes for *Science Now*, claims if the problem is not tackled, plastics in the ocean will triple by 2040. **17** _____ But he reminds everyone it is also up to us as individuals to stop plastic waste.

A The impact of the floods on the seawater had affected its quality.

B Fortunately the scientist was able to remove this by hand using tweezers.

C He ended up at New Brighton Beach on the north coast of New South Wales.

D Plastic debris, smaller than about 5 millimetres, are considered microplastics.

E He had suffered being swept from his home but now an X-ray showed he had a blockage in his colon.

F He sees the international agreement formed to take action to reduce plastic waste across the world as a hopeful sign.

G They harm internal organs as they can't be digested and this causes numerous deaths.

Read the four texts below on the theme of mysteries.

For questions **18–25**, choose the option (**A, B, C** or **D**) which you think best answers the question.

Which text ...

18 does not explain what happened to a named person who is part of the mystery?   _____

19 does not mention research into solving the mystery?   _____

20 refers to similar mysteries within different continents?   _____

21 includes an individual who is optimistic about solving a very old mystery?   _____

22 mentions the explanation for a mystery that is related to change in a species over time?   _____

23 uses recent technologies to prove a much earlier theory likely to be correct?   _____

24 explains why a mystery has led to good news for conservationists?   _____

25 offers the most convincing solution for its mystery?   _____

TEXT A

Good news is to hand about New Zealand's returning sea lions. Previously their numbers were severely reduced by hunters and many were driven south where they settled in subantarctic islands. But now, unexpectedly, they've begun to return. Sea lions tend to breed very close to where they were born so why they are returning now is a mystery to be solved. And even more unexpectedly, they are turning up in places where you'd least expect to see them.

In recent times in New Zealand, there have been several examples of sea lions coming face to face with humans. These include one brave sea lion turning up in a public toilet and another trying to join in a children's soccer game. There are reports of sea lions having to be persuaded out of a community swimming pool and of another who gave birth to her cub right beside the 13th hole on a golf course!

Conservationists are looking to find ways in which humans and sea lions can share their territory more effectively than they have done in the past.

TEXT B

No-one really knows who Big Foot is or even if he really exists. Yet there have been over 10000 recorded sightings of this ape-like creature said to live in the forests of North America. Scientists remain sceptical although some argue it is difficult to ignore the many mysterious tracks that have been found and the thousands of eyewitness accounts.

Yowies, hairy ape-like creatures, have played a similar role in Australia's history. First Australian cultures include stories of a hairy man or yahoo—a large-footed, tall creature—who is sometimes shy but can be violent and aggressive. Sightings have been recorded dating back to early settlement in the 1790s.

Dean Harrison, who has been researching their existence for many years, has set up a website for Australians to note their sightings. He claims to have recorded the sound of the Yowie's roar and to have captured images of them on thermal camera. His images, filmed in the Gold Coast hinterland, are of figures around two metres tall. He believes he's close to confirming their existence.

TEXT C

In November 1872 Captain Benjamin Briggs, his wife and two-year-old daughter, along with seven crew members, left New York on a well fitted-out brigantine, the *Mary Celeste*. They planned to sail to Genoa with a cargo of 1701 barrels of industrial alcohol. They were not short of luxuries: a sewing machine and a piano were on board.

In December 1872 the ship was found adrift on the Atlantic near the Azores. It was quite empty and still perfectly seaworthy. The *Mary Celeste* had become a ghost ship! What could have happened? Where was everybody?

During the 20th century, theories such as attacks by pirates or sea monsters, a possible mutiny or an explosion were put forward as the cause, but none really stood up. Then in the early 21st century, modern scientific techniques were applied to the question. A simulated explosion caused by leaking alcohol was carried out in a replica built of the hold of the ship. Astonishingly, this sent up a wave of flame but left behind no burning or scorching. Mystery solved perhaps?

TEXT D

Inaccessible Island is an extinct volcano rising out of the South Atlantic Ocean. On this remote island, thousands of birds' calls fill the air. They come from rails, the world's smallest flightless birds. How did these flightless birds get on to this island?

Early researchers, who didn't visit the island themselves, were unable to connect the rail to any existing bird species. They thought a possible explanation for its presence on the island could be that, long ago, the island was connected by land bridges to other places. These flightless birds could have reached there by walking. This is now thought to be unlikely; new developments in the science of plate tectonics suggest this is not the way the geography of the area unfolded.

Recent researchers, who have managed to land on the island, have been able to use the rail's DNA to identify their closest relatives. They have confirmed the rail's ancestors were able to fly. It seems the rails must have originally flown to Inaccessible Island and stayed there. A lack of predators meant that over time their ability to fly was unused and, ultimately, lost to them.

SAMPLE TEST 9

Read the text below then answer the questions.

Lenny's Book of Everything

I [Lenore, nicknamed Lenny] named my ladybug Lady and I examined her with a magnifying glass. I examined her glossy back pronotum and her hard-spotted shell. I turned her on her back and examined how perfectly her six legs curled inwards. I knew from the confiscated beetle issue* that she could smell through both her antennae and her feet.

I kept Lady in her jar behind the curtain on the windowsill, but if Mother was in a tidying mood, I hid her in my underpants drawer. I needed to find a fresh supply of aphids each day and I thought she was happy. Each night Davey sat on my bed and said goodnight to the pigeons. Good night, Roger. Good night, Martin, Good night, Frank. We could hear their soft cooing.

He sat on my bed in his striped pyjamas and said, 'I don't think I can sleep.'

'You haven't even tried.'

'Lenny,' he pleaded. 'Len-neeeeeee.'

'What do you want to talk about?'

'Canada,' he said. No hesitation. He meant *imagine it for me*. I was the chief imaginer.

'Okay, picture this,' I said in the dark, and I could hear Davey's breathing shorten in anticipation.

'We go to the train station and we stow away on a train. We take some food and some clothes.'

'What about the books? asked Davey.

'We can't take them with us,' I said. 'That's just ridiculous. You can't run away and take encyclopedias with you.'

'I only mean the one with the African civets and maybe birds,' he said. 'We should take Canada.'

Basically it was every volume we owned so far.

'Okay, I'll think about it,' I said.

'And I'll have Timothy,' said Davey.

I bit my lip in the dark. Davey hadn't told Mother about Lady, so I tried not to make fun of his imaginary golden eagle.

'We could take a balloon,' he said.

'You mean fly in a balloon?' I tried to keep the scorn from my voice.

'Yes,' he whispered.

But then I pictured it. Davey and I clambering into a balloon basket, unhitching the anchor, the sudden uplift, rushing us into the golden morning sky, the city flushed pink below us growing small.

'Where would we find a balloon? I asked. I was the practical one. The sensible one in our running-away stories.

'Maybe they are somewhere,' said Davey. 'They have to be. People have to park balloons somewhere.'

We took a balloon that night. In the darkness of our room.

SAMPLE TEST 9

I said, 'So we find this balloon and we climb into it and off we go. Feel it lift? Up, up, up we go, higher and higher and higher, over the fields and the towns and the cities, all day. And we have our sandwiches and our juice at midday and keep on flying until we reached Great Bear Lake.'

'We'd have to come down sometimes,' said Davey.' 'For more food. Or for the bathroom. You always need the bathroom, Lenny.

'Hush,' I said. 'Don't ruin it.

'Has Mother found us gone yet?'

That jolted the story. We imagined her piecing it together. The sandwich-making crumbs, the missing adventure-type clothes. *A to Ampersand* clearly vanished from the shelf. Amphibians to Aztecs. The bird issue* gone. The balloon faltered in the golden morning sun. Great Bear Lake gleamed far away as perfect as a postcard photo but our balloon snagged itself on a power line. Davey never wore a fur hat. He never strode through the forest with his golden eagle on his shoulder.

It was all talk, but that's how things start.

*instalment of an encyclopedia

From *Lenny's Book of Everything* by Karen Foxlee
© Karen Foxlee; reproduced with permission

For questions **1–6**, choose the answer (**A, B, C** or **D**) which you think best answers the question.

1   What is Lenny's attitude to Lady?

   A distant

   B finicky

   C protective

   D heartless

2   Who is Timothy?

   A a pigeon

   B the ladybug

   C Davey's brother

   D Davey's imaginary friend

3   Canada, in this story, is a place where

   A the children live.

   B the children journey in their imagination.

   C the pigeons like to visit.

   D the children have already been.

4   Which is false? Lenny and Davey

   A share a love of encyclopedia articles.

   B have imaginary friends.

   C are fascinated by animals.

   D are caring of each other.

5   Davey's question, 'Has mother found us gone yet?', 'jolted' the story because

   A it caused their balloon to become caught on a powerline.

   B it made Lenny forget what happened next.

   C Davey needed to visit the bathroom.

   D it shocked them back to reality.

6   The last sentence suggests

   A nothing good will ever come of their dreams.

   B Lenny and Davey see the world differently.

   C making a start can lead to something better.

   D something bad will happen to Davey.

Read the poem below by Robert Frost then answer the questions.

The Road Not Taken

Two roads diverged in a yellow wood,
And sorry I could not travel both
And be one traveller, long I stood
And looked down one as far as I could
To where it bent in the undergrowth;

Then took the other, as just as fair,
And having perhaps the better claim,
Because it was grassy and wanted wear;
Though as for that the passing there
Had worn them really about the same,

And both that morning equally lay
In leaves no step had trodden black.
Oh, I kept the first for another day!
Yet knowing how way leads on to way,
I doubted if I should ever come back.

I shall be telling this with a sigh
Somewhere ages and ages hence:
Two roads diverged in a wood, and I—
I took the one less travelled by,
And that has made all the difference.

For questions **7–11**, choose the answer (**A, B, C** or **D**) which you think best answers the question.

7 The word 'diverged' means

   A united.

   B separated.

   C merged.

   D vanished.

8 The tone of voice used in the poem as a whole is

   A conversational.

   B nervous.

   C anxious.

   D pompous.

9 The speaker claims his choice of road was made

   A randomly.

   B because it had fresh tracks on it.

   C for no particular reason.

   D because it was less travelled.

10 The speaker doubts 'I should ever come back' because he

   A thinks he's grown too old for travel.

   B knows from experience it is unlikely.

   C believes it would be a waste of time.

   D is sure it would be a mistake.

11 The roads in the poem are metaphors for

   A opposing views of the world.

   B attitudes towards change.

   C life's choices

   D the future and the past.

Read the text below then answer the questions.

Six sentences have been removed from the text. Choose from the sentences (**A–G**) the one which fits each gap (**12–17**). There is one extra sentence which you do not need to use.

Fairy rings

A fairy ring can be described as a circular area of grass that is darker in colour than the surrounding grass. **12** _____ Alternatively, the rings may be formed by circular areas of abnormal turf growth.

There are various scientific explanations for fairy rings. Those that are made by mushrooms occur when a mushroom spore falls on a favourable spot. **13** _____ These produce mushroom caps that can continue to expand outwardly. In the Australian outback, where the patches are made of rings of spinifex grass, the cause is less certain. **14** _____ This could encourage new seedlings to gather at the edge where there are fewer pathogens in the soil.

Generally speaking, fairy rings are thought of as magical, mystical places. Some believe they are doorways to other worlds. **15** _____ Some view the mushrooms as table tops on which fairies have their dinner when they gather together.

Most people believe you need to be careful around fairy rings. **16** _____ Another belief is that once inside a ring, humans are forced to dance with fairy creatures until they go mad or die from exhaustion

Beliefs vary from one culture to another. Austrians claim they are made by dragons who burn them into the ground with their fiery tales. The Dutch suggest they are created by the devil as a place to keep his milk churn which turns milk sour for the cattle who come to drink there. **17** _____ They plant their crops around them and believe this will bring them good fortune.

Keep an eye out for fairy rings on your travels. But I wouldn't step inside—just in case!

A   A recent scientific explanation is the possibility that microbes eat away at the older parts of the spinifex.

B   The ring is usually formed by mushrooms that grow in a circular pattern.

C   Fairy forts are the remains of prehistoric stone circles in Ireland.

D   Others assume that the ring is a sign of an underground fairy village.

E   If you step inside, it is thought, you may be in danger of becoming instantly invisible.

F   It builds a network of tubular threads underground in a circular shape.

G   In contrast, the Welsh see the rings as signs of the fertile soil that is nearby.

Read the four texts below on the theme of mothers.

For questions **18–25**, choose the option (**A, B, C** or **D**) which you think best answers the question.

Which text ...

18 is about a mother who provides education for her children? _____

19 reveals a mother who is untrustworthy? _____

20 shows a mother who is less strict than she pretends? _____

21 refers to children who follow in their mother's footsteps? _____

22 uses a conversational, confiding tone? _____

23 shows mounting tension between mother and child? _____

24 includes characters who are stereotypes of good and evil? _____

25 tells why a child admires her mother? _____

TEXT A

Marie Curie, a scientist who won two Nobel Prizes, was the mother of two daughters, Irene and Eve. She lost her own mother to tuberculosis when she was only 11. Sadly her research partner and husband, Pierre, was run over and killed by a horse and carriage soon after the birth of their second daughter.

When living in Paris, Marie was dissatisfied with the schooling available and took on the responsibility for the education of her daughters. She organised a group of nine children, including her own, to have lessons from specialists in a wide range of subjects.

When Irene was 17, she was rewarded with military honours for helping soldiers during the war. Later she and her husband received the Nobel prize for their research into radioactivity. Eve also led a useful, successful life. She was nominated for a Pulitzer Prize for her writing and actively did humanitarian work for many years with UNICEF, an organisation that aims to save children's lives and defend their rights.

TEXT B

My mum's name is Peggy. She said this nickname was given to her because she has a peg-top nose. I reckon she had a sad beginning to her life. She was brought up by her uncles and aunts. One of her uncles was a music teacher and the other trained horses. The stay-at-home aunties managed as best they could. Mum told me she often got into trouble and would hide in a cupboard until they'd forgive her.

I feel sad she couldn't be what she wanted to be when she grew up. She wanted to be a ballerina but her family couldn't afford the lessons. She still does the splits on the kitchen floor every now and then.

Mum is never afraid of doing what she thinks is right. She's very brave in that way, I think. Braver than I am, let me tell you! I hope I can be more like her when I grow up.

SAMPLE TEST 9

TEXT C

'Can I have my dinner, mother?' he [William] cried, rushing in with his cap on. ' 'Cause it begins at half-past one, the man says so.'

'You can have your dinner as soon as it's done,' replied the mother.

'Isn't it done?' he cried, his blue eyes staring at her in indignation. 'Then I'm goin' be-out it.'

'You'll do nothing of the sort. It will be done in five minutes. It is only half-past twelve.'

'They'll be beginnin',' the boy half cried, half shouted.

'You won't die if they do,' said the mother. 'Besides, it's only half-past twelve, so you've a full hour.'

[...]

Some distance away could be heard the first small braying of a merry-go-round, and the tooting of a horn. His face quivered as he looked at his mother.

'I told you!' he said, running to the dresser for his cap.

'Take your pudding in your hand—and it's only five past one, so you were wrong—you haven't got your twopence,' cried the mother in a breath.

From *Sons and Lovers* by DH Lawrence

TEXT D

Then Ashputtel brought the dish to her mother, overjoyed at the thought that now she should go to the ball. But the mother said, 'No, no! you have no clothes, and cannot dance; you shall not go.' And when Ashputtel begged very hard to go, she said, 'If you can in one hour's time pick two of those dishes of peas out of the ashes, you shall go too.' And thus she thought she should at least get rid of her. So she shook two dishes of peas into the ashes.

But the little maiden went out into the garden at the back of the house, and cried out as before:

> 'Hither, hither, through the sky,
> Turtle-doves and linnets, fly!
> Blackbird, thrush, and chaffinch gay,
> Hither, hither, haste away!
> One and all come help me, quick!
> Haste ye, haste ye!—pick, pick, pick!'

Before half an hour's time all was done, and out they flew again. And then Ashputtel took the dishes to her mother, rejoicing to think that she should now go to the ball. But her mother said, 'It is all of no use, you cannot go; you have no clothes, and cannot dance, and you would only put us to shame': and off she went with her two daughters to the ball.

From 'Ashputtel', *Grimm's Fairy Tales*

Read the text below then answer the questions.

The Garden

'What a curious feeling!' said Alice; 'I must be shutting up like a telescope.'

And so it was indeed: she was now only ten inches high, and her face brightened up at the thought that she was now the right size for going through the little door into that lovely garden. First, however, she waited for a few minutes to see if she was going to shrink any further: she felt a little nervous about this; 'for it might end, you know,' said Alice to herself, 'in my going out altogether, like a candle. I wonder what I should be like then?' And she tried to fancy what the flame of a candle is like after the candle is blown out, for she could not remember ever having seen such a thing.

After a while, finding that nothing more happened, she decided on going into the garden at once; but, alas for poor Alice! when she got to the door, she found she had forgotten the little golden key, and when she went back to the table for it, she found she could not possibly reach it: she could see it quite plainly through the glass, and she tried her best to climb up one of the legs of the table, but it was too slippery; and when she had tired herself out with trying, the poor little thing sat down and cried.

'Come, there's no use in crying like that!' said Alice to herself, rather sharply; 'I advise you to leave off this minute!' She generally gave herself very good advice, (though she very seldom followed it), and sometimes she scolded herself so severely as to bring tears into her eyes; and once she remembered trying to box her own ears for having cheated herself in a game of croquet she was playing against herself, for this curious child was very fond of pretending to be two people. 'But it's no use now,' thought poor Alice, 'to pretend to be two people! Why, there's hardly enough of me left to make *one* respectable person!'

Soon her eye fell on a little glass box that was lying under the table: she opened it, and found in it a very small cake, on which the words 'EAT ME' were beautifully marked in currants. 'Well, I'll eat it,' said Alice, 'and if it makes me grow larger, I can reach the key; and if it makes me grow smaller, I can creep under the door; so either way I'll get into the garden, and I don't care which happens!'

She ate a little bit, and said anxiously to herself, 'Which way? Which way?', holding her hand on the top of her head to feel which way it was growing, and she was quite surprised to find that she remained the same size: to be sure, this generally happens when one eats cake, but Alice had got so much into the way of expecting nothing but out-of-the-way things to happen, that it seemed quite dull and stupid for life to go on in the common way.

So she set to work, and very soon finished off the cake.

****

'Curiouser and curiouser!' cried Alice (she was so much surprised, that for the moment she quite forgot how to speak good English); 'now I'm opening out like the largest telescope that ever was! Good-bye, feet!' (for when she looked down at her feet, they seemed to be almost out of sight, they were getting so far off). 'Oh, my poor little feet, I wonder who will put on your shoes and stockings for you now, dears? I'm sure *I* shan't be able! I shall be a great deal too far off to trouble myself about you: you must manage the best way you can; — but I must be kind to them,' thought Alice, 'or perhaps they won't walk the way I want to go! Let me see: I'll give them a new pair of boots every Christmas.'

And she went on planning to herself how she would manage it. 'They must go by the carrier,' she thought; 'and how funny it'll seem, sending presents to one's own feet! And how odd the directions will look!

> *Alice's Right Foot, Esq.,*
> *Hearthrug,*
> *near the Fender,*
> *(with Alice's love).*

Oh dear, what nonsense I'm talking!'

Just then her head struck against the roof of the hall: in fact she was now more than nine feet high, and she at once took up the little golden key and hurried off to the garden door.

Poor Alice! It was as much as she could do, lying down on one side, to look through into the garden with one eye; but to get through was more hopeless than ever: she sat down and began to cry again.

'You ought to be ashamed of yourself,' said Alice, 'a great girl like you,' (she might well say this), 'to go on crying in this way! Stop this moment, I tell you!' But she went on all the same, shedding gallons of tears, until there was a large pool all round her, about four inches deep and reaching half down the hall.

From *Alice's Adventures in Wonderland* by Lewis Carroll

For questions **1–6**, choose the answer (**A, B, C** or **D**) which you think best answers the question.

1 Alice is pleased to have shrunk because she

A no longer feels nervous.

B dislikes being tall.

C thinks now she'll be able to get into the garden.

D likes the feeling of shutting up like a telescope.

2 The main reason Alice begins to cry is

A she lost a game of croquet.

B she can't climb up the table leg.

C she had forgotten she needed the key.

D she still can't get into the garden.

3 When the author uses the word 'curious' to describe Alice he means she is

A special.

B eager.

C inquisitive.

D unusual.

4 What does Alice mean when she asks 'Which way? Which way?'?

A Which direction will take me to the garden?

B In which direction should I turn?

C Am I growing smaller or taller after eating the cake?

D Should I eat more or less of the cake?

5 Alice's reaction to finding her feet far away mainly adds _____ to the story.

A humour   B intrigue

C tension   D horror

6 The author adds '(she might well say this)' in the last paragraph to

A show his approval.

B point out the humour of what Alice says.

C disagree with Alice's point of view.

D point out that Alice is quite grown up.

Read the poem by Sheryl Persson then answer the questions.

Cockatoo Island, at the junction of rivers in Sydney Harbour, belonged to the Eora people, was a penal settlement, was blasted and excavated, has a history as an official dockyard and is now open to the public.

Cockatoo Island

These days, the salt of Sydney Harbour mixes
a freshwater Parramatta River cocktail
as a river cat creeps, sweeps in
rubs and scratches the Cockatoo Island wharf
The crowd in slow motion morning
shuffles off to set up camp, wander in the past
others, city bound sail on towards skyline
and the arching bridge
Visitors dwarfed by rusting remnants of
    industry
a new tribe, where once
the spirit ancestors of the Wangal people
fished in the time of a different dreaming
This island of many incarnations
inhabited by too many nameless ghosts
sulphur-cresteds scarce now, a phalanx of
    cranes
stand like titan birds, beaks ready to peck prey
Its own massive art installation, cliffs cut away
the grand scale of brick, iron, sandstone
where Norfolk convicts toiled, turbines
    roared
Voyager, Vampire and an Empress came into
    being
The past echoes through empty workshops,
    cells, slipways
but if all those stories were declaimed together
a cacophony of deafening voices
would haunt the casual tourists   send them
    packing

© Sheryl Persson; reproduced with permission

For questions 7–11, choose the answer (**A, B, C** or **D**) which you think best answers the question.

7 What 'scratches' the Cockatoo Island wharf?

A a cat

B salt from the river

C water

D a ferry

8 The 'rusting remnants of industry' on the island refer to

A the convicts.

B the leftover bits of decaying constructions.

C the ghosts who visit.

D the arching bridge.

9 The cranes are compared to 'titan birds' mainly because they

A hop about and peck at crumbs.

B look similar to sulphur-crested cockatoos.

C look like giant birds with long dangerous beaks.

D are a new breed of crane.

10 'Voyager, Vampire and an Empress' are most likely to be

A birds.   B ships.

C machines.   D ghosts.

11 The 'deafening voices' the poet imagines are made by

A nameless ghosts. B the crowd.

C visitors.   D casual tourists.

SAMPLE TEST 10

Read the text below then answer the questions.

Six sentences have been removed from the text. Choose from the sentences (**A–G**) the one which fits each gap (**12–17**). There is one extra sentence which you do not need to use.

Australian Children's Laureates

A laureate is a person who is officially honoured with an award for outstanding achievement. **12** _____ Traditionally the leaves of the bay tree (*Laurus nobilis*) were woven into a crown to be worn as a sign of victory.

In modern times, many countries have recognised achievements by awarding the title of laureate. **13** _____ There are currently Children's Laureates in Australia, Ireland, The Netherlands, the United Kingdom, Mexico, Sweden, the USA and Wales.

The Australian Children's Laureate Foundation introduced the award of Australian Children's Laureate. **14** _____ It was chosen because it is a bird known for its striking appearance, its beautiful voice, its fierce protection of the young and the fact it can fly! It is a biennial award and was first given in 2012.

The award for 2012 to 2013 was shared by two people: Alison Lester and Boori Monty Pryor. **15** _____ During her laureateship, as well as promoting reading, she encouraged children to create stories of their own about their own special place.

Boori Monty Pryor is a First Australian descended from the Birri Gubba and the Yarrabah nations of Queensland. **16** _____ He has won multiple awards for his books including for *The Binna Binna Man* and *Shake a Leg*. You can find him reading *Story Doctors* (2021) in Gunggandji and English online as he continues to promote the importance of storytelling.

Ursula Dubosarsky was the Australian Children's Laureate for 2020 to 2021. Ursula has written over 60 books to national and international acclaim. The theme of Ursula's laureateship was 'Read for Your Life'. She encouraged the idea that every child should have their own library card.

At the ceremony, when Ursula was given her crown of laurel leaves and magpie statuette, she asked children from the audience to act out a story. **17** _____ The littlest ant chooses a storybook. 'What good is that?' scoffs the Chief Ant. The story has since been made into a picture book, *The March of the Ants*, illustrated by Tohby Riddle. If you don't know how the story ends, perhaps you could borrow it from your local library?

A   For example, there are Nobel Laureates and Poet Laureates.

B   Reading changes lives.

C   Their logo is the Australian magpie.

D   Alison has written over 30 books including well-known titles such as *Ernie Dances to the Didgeridoo* and *Are We There Yet?*

E   The story was about ants going on an important expedition with each taking something useful for their journey.

F   It comes from the Latin word *laureatus* meaning 'crowned with a laurel wreath'.

G   He is a performer: a storyteller, a didgeridoo player, a dancer, a public speaker and a filmmaker.

Read the four texts below on the theme of feelings.

For questions **18–25**, choose the option (**A, B, C** or **D**) which you think best answers the question.

Which text ...

18 includes characters who express anger? _____

19 refers to the idea of not showing your feelings? _____

20 explains why someone feels joyful? _____

21 shows how a feeling can turn into a violent action? _____

22 ends on a note of hope? _____

23 mentions sadness that won't go away? _____

24 describes the least intense feelings? _____

25 is about someone who feels excluded? _____

TEXT A

Heidi led her friend to her favourite spot where she was accustomed to sit and enjoy the beauty around her; the doctor followed her example and took his seat beside her on the warm grass. The great snowfield sparkled in the bright sunlight, on the rocky peaks. A soft, light morning breeze blew deliciously across the mountain, gently stirring the bluebells that still remained of the summer's wealth of flowers, their slender heads nodding cheerfully in the sunshine. Overhead the great bird was flying round and round in wide circles. Heidi looked about her first at one thing and then at another. Her eyes were alight with joy. She turned to her friend to see if he too were enjoying the beauty. The doctor had been sitting thoughtfully gazing around him. As he met her glad bright eyes, 'Yes, Heidi,' he responded, 'I see how lovely it all is, but tell me—if one brings a sad heart up here, how may it be healed so that it can rejoice in all this beauty?'

From *Heidi* by Johanna Spyri

TEXT B

Gilbert reached across the aisle, picked up the end of Anne's long red braid, held it out at arm's length and said in a piercing whisper:

'Carrots! Carrots!'

Then Anne looked at him with a vengeance!

She did more than look. She sprang to her feet, her bright fancies fallen into cureless ruin. She flashed one indignant glance at Gilbert from eyes whose angry sparkle was swiftly quenched in equally angry tears.

'You mean, hateful boy!' she exclaimed passionately. 'How dare you!'

And then—thwack! Anne had brought her slate down on Gilbert's head and cracked it—slate not head—clear across.

[...]

Mr Phillips stalked down the aisle and laid his hand heavily on Anne's shoulder.

'Anne Shirley, what does this mean?' he said angrily.

From *Anne of Green Gables* by LM Montgomery

TEXT C

'What happened to Rebecca at the swimming carnival?' Jack asked.

'She slipped and broke her wrist,' Ellie said.

'That was bad luck.'

'By the way, Jack, good on you for winning your race.'

'Thanks, Ellie,' Jack said with a happy smile.

There was a crowd gathered around Rebecca in the classroom. She had a shiny white plaster on her left arm.

'Can I sign your plaster?'

'Let me!' came the cries.

'Later,' Rebecca answered.

When the bell went for morning tea, Rebecca went over to Ellie.

'Will you sign my plaster, Ellie, please?' Ellie picked up her pen, wrote her name and added some smiley faces to make it look cheerful. Thank goodness, she thought. Their quarrel was over. They were friends again. Perhaps, someday, they might even be *good* friends.

From *Just Good Friends* by Donna Gibbs
© Donna Gibbs; reproduced with permission

TEXT D

But what were Molly's feelings at these last words of her father's? She had been sent from home for some reason, kept a secret from her, but told to this strange woman. Was there to be perfect confidence between these two, and she to be for ever shut out?.

[...]

She was positively unhappy, and her father did not appear to see it; he was absorbed with his new plans and his new wife that was to be. But he did notice it; and was truly sorry for his little girl: only he thought that there was a greater chance for the future harmony of the household, if he did not lead Molly to define her present feelings by putting them into words. It was his general plan to repress emotion by not showing the sympathy he felt.

[...]

Molly had held up all the day bravely; she had not shown anger, or repugnance, or annoyance, or regret; but when once more by herself in the Hamley carriage, she burst into a passion of tears.

From *Wives and Daughters* by Elizabeth Gaskell

MINI **Test 1**

Page 1

1 C 2 D 3 B

1　It is the silence and the stern expressions on his friends' faces that alarm Toad and cause him to stumble over his invitation.

A is incorrect. There is no evidence that Toad is shy. In fact, he tends to be confident and outspoken.

B is incorrect. At this stage his friends are not paying attention to his car.

D is incorrect. Although noticing his friends' silence is part of why Toad stumbles over his invitation, it is the combination of his friends' silence and stern expressions that cause him to stumble and then stop speaking altogether.

2　Badger makes every effort to be fair to Toad. His crimes sound quite serious—'furious driving', 'smashes' and 'rows with the police'—so it is clear he needs to be firmly corrected. The decision to give Toad a second chance by his friends is more than reasonable.

A is incorrect. There is no evidence that Badger's criticisms are unjustified.

B is incorrect. It takes courage to confront Toad with unpleasant truths about his behaviour and character.

C is incorrect. There is no evidence of cruelty from Badger—just plain speaking about Toad's poor behaviour.

3　You can work out that Rat thinks Toad will promise Badger he will reform but will fail to change his behaviour. He doesn't have any faith in what Toad says he will do. Hence Rat is highly scornful of the likely success of Badger's plan to take Toad aside for a private talk.

A and C are incorrect. There is no evidence that Rat thinks Badger's plan will be successful in any way.

D is incorrect. Although feeling annoyed is part of Rat's reaction, the word doesn't convey the strength of how he feels, which is contemptuous and scornful.

MINI **Test 2**

Page 4

1 D 2 B

1　The story is told from beginning to end by the poet. Conversations between the Spider and the Fly are included as part of the narration.

A and B are incorrect. Although both the Spider and the Fly speak in the poem, the story as a whole is told by the poet.

C is incorrect. The 'evil counsellor' is an imaginary figure that the poet warns children about.

2　The moral of the poem is to beware of flattery. The Fly's vanity leads it to be flattered by the Spider into doing things that lead to its death. Very unwise!

A and C are incorrect. The meanings of these sayings have no similarity with the moral of the poem.

D is incorrect. Although this mentions flattery it is about a form flattery can take, not about its dangers.

MINI **Test 3**

Page 6

1 C 2 A 3 B

1　In the previous sentence the author describes the attitude of governments to First Australians in the 1950s. This sentence gives evidence of this: It was not until 1961 that all First Australians were given the right to vote, for example. The sentence that follows describes an attitude in the local community that reflects this attitude.

2　In the previous sentence the author refers to Evonne's passion for ball games. This sentence gives evidence of this: The story goes that a lucky find of a tennis ball under the wheel of her father's car kept her happily occupied for long stretches of time. The sentence that follows tells how her father gave her a wooden racquet so she could enjoy playing 'tennis' with her ball.

3 In the previous sentence the author notes that in 2009 Barellan, Evonne's hometown, celebrated its centenary. This sentence describes one of the ways they celebrated: Part of their celebrations involved the building of 'The Big Tennis Racquet'. The sentence that follows gives more detail about what the racquet looked like.

The unused sentence is D.

MINI Test 4
Page 7

1 C 2 B 3 A 4 B

1 The author points out that if we change our behaviour, such as by using less plastic, then the health of our oceans will improve.

A and B are incorrect. They are not about changing what people do in relation to the health of oceans.

2 This text gives a scientific account of how oceans were formed and outlines each of the processes believed to have taken place.

A and D are incorrect. They do not address the question of how oceans were formed.

3 The author's description of the ocean as it unrolls, crashes, arches and falls against the rocks, and its magical colours in the sunset—the bluey grass-green and the snow-pure rush of foam of its waves—suggest the author's admiration of its power and beauty.

B is incorrect. It tells how oceans are formed in a detached, scientific way.

C is incorrect. It expresses the author's pressing concern for the health of our oceans rather than awe of any kind.

4 The author states there is 70% of water on the earth's surface. This implies there is 30% land—a much smaller amount.

A and B are incorrect. They don't make comparisons between the amount of land and water on the earth's surface.

SAMPLE Test 1
Page 1

1 A 2 C 3 D 4 B 5 C 6 A 7 B 8 C 9 C
10 A 11 B 12 B 13 G 14 A 15 E 16 D
17 F 18 C 19 A 20 D 21 C 22 D 23 A
24 B 25 D

1 Jerusha labels the day with a title in capitals (Perfectly Awful Day) as a way of making light of her heavy responsibilities. She knows she shouldn't think about the Trustees' visit in that way but that is exactly how she sees it. Having the charge of 97 little orphans, not to mention cleaning and making sandwiches on the first Wednesday of every month, is a herculean task!

B and C are incorrect. There is no evidence the trustees or the other orphans find the day 'Perfectly Awful' in the way Jerusha does.

D is incorrect. The label with its capitals refers to a particular day of the month and not life in the orphanage more generally.

2 Jerusha has always lived at the orphanage and has never had a home of her own. She can imagine herself dressed up and driving in a carriage but her imagination falters when she reaches the doorsill of her imaginary home. She just can't envisage having a home that belongs to her.

A is incorrect. Although she is exhausted from her day, this is not what prevents her from imagining a home of her own.

B is incorrect. There is no rain mentioned and even if there was rain, it wouldn't blur her imagination.

D is incorrect. Her thoughts blur before she hears Tommy calling to her.

3 Tommy has just joined the choir and adapts the rhythm of the message for Jerusha to make it into a chant. He cheekily adds the traditional ending of a hymn or prayer: Amen.

A and B are incorrect. Tommy has good control of each word of his message and neither stumbles nor stutters.

C is incorrect. Mrs Lippett is in the office and not in a place where she is likely to hear Tommy.

4 Jerusha finds the Trustee's transformation from actual gentleman to a huge, wavering daddy-long-legs, in the form of a shadow, very amusing.

A is incorrect. While it is true Jerusha doesn't have a habit of frowning, this is not what causes her to laugh.

C and D are incorrect. They don't match the sequence of events. Jerusha has left Tommy behind upstairs when she laughs (C) and Mrs Lippett has not yet told her she has read her 'Blue Wednesday' paper (D).

5 Mrs Lippett finds it hard to believe that an 'impertinent' paper that showed ridicule and ingratitude towards the orphanage would be the cause of a Trustee's decision to offer its author a reward.

A is incorrect. Although Mrs Lippett recognises the gentleman Trustee has an 'immoderate' sense of humour, it is what this leads him to do as a result that is more surprising to her.

B is incorrect. Mrs Lippett is well aware Jerusha has outgrown her time at the orphanage and will need to do something different in her future.

D is incorrect. Jerusha does have a reaction: her eyes grow big and Mrs Lippett is aware of this.

6 Although Mrs Lippett speaks slowly and placidly to Jerusha, her tone and the words she chooses (such as 'impertinent') reveal a fair degree of disapproval of Jerusha's behaviour.

B and C are incorrect. They describe tones that carry much stronger degrees of disapproval than are evident in Mrs Lippett's words.

D is incorrect. Mrs Lippett states her disapproval of Jerusha's written paper so her tone cannot be described as non-judgemental.

7 The poet says he can't remember anything connected to the death of his horse: the when, the how or the where it died.

A is incorrect. He doesn't say he can't remember what the horse looked like.

C is incorrect. He recalls, for example, his mare's wilful behaviour.

D is incorrect. The poet wonders what might have caused his horse to die but doesn't reach any conclusion about it.

8 The thought of the mare being helped to a painless death is what the poet likes to imagine happening to his horse at the end.

A is incorrect. He doesn't imagine his recovery.

B is incorrect. He has already imagined the mare's hectic blood being tamed as it grew older and this takes place before the vet's visit.

D is incorrect. Although he may know of his family's trust in the vet, this is not what he is referring to when he describes what he 'likes to think'.

9 The poet speculates about what happened to his mare at the end of her life and implies she may have been taken to an abattoir on a lorry with other cattle.

The other options are incorrect. The poet doesn't imply any specific way his mare's life may have been taken (i.e. being shot, drugged or poisoned) other than that she may have shared the same fate as cattle who are taken away from their home in a lorry.

10 The word 'munching' suggests a pleasurable experience and munching through 'a last few summers' indicates the mare is unhurried and is lazily at peace.

The other options are incorrect. The mare is munching slowly through its last years, not greedily snatching at food, showing distress or being wasteful.

11 The poet wonders about the when, how and where of his mare's death and imagines what might have happened to her at the last.

A is incorrect. The poet wants to believe his family would have done the right thing by the horse. He is more puzzled than annoyed.

C is incorrect. There is a tone of acceptance that these events are in the past and not something he can do anything about.

D is incorrect. Although he may have loved his mare with a passion and regrets not being with her when she died, his tone throughout the poem is reflective rather than passionate.

12 In the previous sentence the author asks if the reader is aware lychees are a popular part of Lunar New Year celebrations. This sentence tells when that celebration takes place: This spring-time festival begins on 1 February and lasts until 15 February each year. The sentence that follows tells where and by whom the festival is celebrated.

13 In the previous sentence the author says lychees are associated with Lunar New Year celebrations. This sentence points out lychees are traditionally used in a particular way in these celebrations: It is traditional to make decorative wreaths with their branches. The sentence that follows names other ways they are included in the Festival.

14 In the previous sentence the author says the Knoblock family were unaware of the part lychees played in Lunar traditions. This sentence points out they originally had different plans for their farm: When they arrived at their new home, they planned to grow snow peas. The sentence that follows reports they changed their mind about this.

15 In the previous sentence the author says the family taught themselves how to cultivate lychees. This sentence points out the result they achieved: Today their lychee farm covers three hectares. The sentence that follows tells what kind of lychees they produce on their farm.

16 In the previous sentence the author says there are many factors that affect the time for harvesting lychees. This sentence names two of these factors: These include climate and the location of the trees. The sentence that follows provides examples of different harvest times in locations in two Australian states to illustrate this point.

17 In the previous sentence the author says the Knoblocks allow visitors to pick their own lychees. This sentence explains what happens after they have completed their picking: After this they weigh and pay for them. The sentence that follows adds another detail about the process: visitors are allowed to eat the lychees for free while they are picking them.

The unused sentence is C.

18 Zyrgon is a fictional planet, occupied by aliens, referred to in this text.

A and B are incorrect. These texts do not refer to fictional planets.

D is incorrect. The planets mentioned exist in space and time.

19 The story included in this text is about the importance of taking notice of your elders. It illustrates the idea that ignoring what your elders say can have dangerous consequences.

The other options are incorrect. These texts do not contain stories with morals.

20 This text provides information about scientific research currently being carried out on Mars, a planet that is the most likely to accommodate humans in the future.

A is incorrect. The information in this text is not scientific.

B and C are incorrect. The information included in these texts is not shown to be related to the earth's future.

21 The aliens, who are not part of human society, see earth from a different perspective from humans. They find it hard to fit in when they visit earth and they question the choices humans make.

The other options are incorrect. These texts do not offer a view of human behaviour on planet earth from the perspective of outsiders.

22 The information about planets Venus and Mars is interspersed with personal comments, including jokes, made to Riley by his grandmother.

The other options are incorrect. They do not include personal comments.

23 Aboriginal star maps, which follow traditions from an ancient culture, are compared with modern ways of mapping.

The other options are incorrect. These texts do not compare ancient and modern cultures.

24 The writer gives an account of how astrologers make their predictions but points out that their methods have no scientific validity.

The other options are incorrect. The writers of these texts are confident in the validity of their information.

25 Riley's grandmother says she has been studying astronomy. She passes on some of the facts she has learned about the planets to Riley.

A and C are incorrect. These texts do not include information that is scientifically proven.

B is incorrect. Although the information in this text may have been learned from private study, the source of this information is not stated.

SAMPLE Test 2 Page 16

1 C 2 A 3 B 4 D 5 D 6 C 7 C 8 B 9 C
10 D 11 B 12 C 13 D 14 G 15 B 16 A
17 E 18 B 19 A 20 D 21 C 22 B 23 A
24 D 25 C

1 When Mowgli is sighted by the village boys they shout and run away, which implies his appearance threatens them in some way.

A is incorrect. Although it is true Mowgli can jog-trot for long distances, this suggests his physical strength and resilience, not what he looks like to the boys.

B is incorrect. How Mowgli speaks is not relevant to his appearance.

D is incorrect. Mowgli frowns at the crowd, not at the boys, and a frown would not necessarily mean he looks different.

2 The priest is cunning and knows Messua is from a wealthy family. He knows Messua would love to have a son and so he pretends he knows Mowgli is her rightful gift. He suggests she honour him, which is his way of asking to be paid for his blessing.

B is incorrect. It may be true that the priest wants Messua to get over her sorrow but this is less important to him than securing payment from her.

C is incorrect. There is no evidence as to what the priest believes.

D is incorrect. Although the priest claims to see far into the lives of men, there is no evidence that he can do so. He claims this to justify his request for a reward for his services.

3 Mowgli considers the behaviour of the menfolk, who stare, shout and point at him, uncivil and rude.

A and C are incorrect. Mowgli doesn't show any fear of the crowd.

D is incorrect. Mowgli doesn't show any interest in attacking the crowd.

4 When Messua feels Mowgli's feet she can tell from the hardness of his feet that he has never worn shoes, whereas she knows her son has worn shoes. This convinces her he is not her son who was taken by a tiger.

A is incorrect. Although Messua sees Mowgli's scars, this does not prove to her he is not her son.

B is incorrect. Although Messua sees Mowgli is skinny, she still thinks he could be her son.

C is incorrect. Messua still thinks he might be her son after she looks into his eyes.

5 Once Mowgli realises he can easily escape from Messua's hut, he is willing to stay there for a time.

A is incorrect. Mowgli shows no interest in these objects and they would have no value for him.

B is incorrect. Although Mowgli is hungry and wants food, he is too smart to stay in the hut without having an escape route.

C is incorrect. There is no evidence Mowgli seeks to be loved by Messua.

6   Mowgli recognises that, as a man, he needs to know the language of men.

A is incorrect. There is no evidence Mowgli wants to escape from the wolves.

B is incorrect. Mowgli shows no interest in pleasing the priest.

D is incorrect. Mowgli shows no interest in belonging to anyone.

7   The narrator is excusing her parents for their choice of name for her by suggesting it must have felt like the right choice to them.

A is incorrect. The narrator's feelings are not something her parents could have known about.

B is incorrect. Where her mum was the night before her birth did influence the choice of name but doesn't provide an excuse for it.

D is incorrect. Although it offers some consolation for the choice (she turned out partly like the person she was named after) it does not offer an excuse that frees the parents from blame.

8   The narrator doesn't associate her name with a person like herself. She can't imagine herself as the person that name suggests.

A is incorrect. Although her not wanting to be associated with a movie star may be part of her reason, there is more to her dislike of the name than that.

C is incorrect. There is no evidence she feels her parents wanted to punish her.

D is incorrect. Although she feels she doesn't live up to the person who is her namesake in terms of beauty, this is only part of the reaction she has to her name.

9   To know how to 'google' or use a search engine to find information on the internet is evidence of being a competent internet user but nothing further can be assumed from her having this ability other than, perhaps, she must live in the 20th or 21st century.

The other options are incorrect. They could all be true, however!

10   The narrator confides the story of what led to her not changing her name in a personal, direct way as though she is having a conversation with her audience.

A is incorrect. The tone is not formal as it includes casual expressions (So there!; Anyway) and slang (publicity guy).

B is incorrect. Although there is an element of childishness in places, the poem as a whole is conversational rather than childish.

C is incorrect. The narrator doesn't convey anger but rather discomfort and unease.

11   The narrator can't bring herself to give a name that isn't her real name when the time comes. Her body language conveys the trouble she has when trying to tell a lie.

A is incorrect. While she shows signs of embarrassment (stuttering, blushing), it is not suggested she feels unhappy with the new name she has chosen.

C and D are incorrect. There is no evidence that she prefers her real name or that she is confused about what to say.

12   In the previous sentence the author explains what tattoos are. This sentence tells how they can be added to the skin: This can be done through inserting dye or ink in a way that leaves a permanent mark or pattern. The sentence that follows provides another way this can be achieved: through impermanent markings.

13   In the previous sentence the author lists various designs used in tattoos. This sentence points out that tattoos are also used for various purposes: The purposes for which they are used within a culture also vary. The

sentence that follows lists some of these purposes.

14 In the previous sentence the author states that traditional sailors used tattoos to give information about their status and marine experiences. This sentence gives an example of a tattoo used to indicate status: A boatswain, for example, wore crossed anchors on the webbing between thumb and index finger to indicate status. The sentence that follows gives examples of tattoos that indicate other achievements made by sailors.

15 In the previous sentence the author gives an example of tattoos sailors had because of superstition. This sentence provides another example of a tattoo related to a superstition: A star was also worn for superstitious reasons. The sentence that follows gives more information about the origins of this superstition.

16 In the previous sentence the author states that not all cultures approve of tattoos. This sentence gives an example of a culture that has considered tattoos taboo: In Japan, for example, at least until recently, people have been banned from beaches, swimming pools and other public areas if they wear body art. The sentence that follows provides an explanation for this attitude.

17 In the previous sentence the author refers to the type of tattoos popular in modern societies. This sentence explains what has led to their popularity: Their popularity has been encouraged by social media where celebrities, athletes and others sport them in public view. The sentence that follows explains that a version of tattooing that is temporary rather than permanent is increasing in popularity.

The unused sentence is F.

18 The tone the author uses to point out the extraordinary achievements of scientists in being able to measure things that can't be seen with the human eye is very respectful.

A is incorrect. It expresses awe for the achievements of those in the 'race' rather than respect for the researchers who measure the speeds achieved.

C and D are incorrect. These texts are not about the achievements of scientists.

19 This is a news item spoken to an audience of listeners. The language is relaxed and informal (the king of speed; blow that record out of the water) and has a conversational tone. It compresses ideas in a catchy, unscientific way (Robots comes to mind.). It signals it has come to an end by saying 'And now to the weather'.

B and D are incorrect. These texts do not have the features of a spoken text.

C is incorrect. Although it includes conversation, this is part of a written story.

20 Usain Bolt's speed records are included as part of his achievements in a short biographical account of his life.

The other options are incorrect. These texts do not include biographical information.

21 The fable about the tortoise and the hare implies that slow and steady wins the race and speed is not everything.

The other options are incorrect. These texts are not said or written with the purpose of illustrating a moral.

22 This text provides a definition of speed with examples that illustrate its meaning. Its language is precise and includes some technical terms (scalar; numerical value) making it suitable for inclusion in a scientific text.

The other options are incorrect because they do not have the form or type of language suitable for this purpose.

23 This news item includes the comment that further research into how speed is achieved in animals could lead to discoveries that provide helpful products for humans.

B is incorrect. It does not mention outcomes of future research.

C and D are incorrect. These texts are not about research.

24 Details about Bolt's childhood and the names of his children, for example, are personal details.

The other options are incorrect. These texts do not include personal information.

25 The fable about the tortoise and the hare includes a fox who acts as a judge in charge of setting up conditions for the race and announcing its winner.

A and B are incorrect. While the animals mentioned take part in the experiments, they do not make judgements about the results.

D is incorrect. There are no animals referred to in this text.

SAMPLE **Test 3**

Page 22

1 B 2 A 3 B 4 C 5 B 6 D 7 B 8 D 9 C
10 B 11 C 12 C 13 F 14 D 15 A 16 B
17 G 18 C 19 B 20 D 21 A 22 D 23 A
24 B 25 C

1 The Aviator enables Kate to visit a time when Ned Kelly was alive, which makes it some kind of time-travel machine.

The other options are incorrect. None of these forms of transport involve time travel, which is an essential part of the Aviator's function.

2 Kate has learned the Aviator is controlled by the power of the mind. She realises that concentrating on a particular time period and place is the way to get to where she wants to be in the past. She refers to this knowledge immediately after her comment about it not being a good idea to lose concentration.

B is incorrect. There are no instructions written on the machine.

C is incorrect. Although losing concentration could lead to her being caught by Sam's father, there is no evidence she is thinking about Sam's father.

D is incorrect. Although this might happen, there is no evidence Kate sees this as a possibility.

3 Time travel is not possible in our present world, which means a story that treats this phenomenon as reality is in fact a fantasy.

A and D are incorrect. Although there may be hints of mystery and romance in the story, these are ephemeral and not related to its overall type or genre.

C is incorrect. Although a crime is referred to in the story (a bank robbery by the Kelly gang) and it is a real historical event, Kate being at the scene of a crime in 1878 is part of a larger fantasy.

4 Kate is present at the aftermath of the Kelly gang's robbery of the National Bank in 1878. She describes a rural Australian setting in Victoria but even if you don't know the location in Australia you can work out this is the only answer that meets the criteria.

A and D are incorrect. The date of the bank robbery is 1878, which is a time in the 19th century.

B is incorrect. The setting is described in terms of rural Australia: a Station homestead, bush picnic, and so on.

5 Kate includes conversational expressions (dead scared; on track; Not such a good idea!) throughout the telling of her story. She is very involved with the events and shares her personal feelings and reactions.

A is incorrect. Kate's personal responses to events are very evident.

C is incorrect. Kate is curious and observant rather than critical about what is happening in her world.

D is incorrect. Although there is a touch of humour in Kate's account of the effect Ned Kelly has upon her, the rest of the telling is more serious.

6 The most likely reason Ned suggests Kate be given a glass of water is that he thinks she looks dizzy and as though she might faint. Kate confirms she does feel dizzy although she attributes her dizziness to the tightness of her corset. (The reader assumes it also has to do with the experience of looking into Ned's eyes and hearing him call her 'Blondie'.).

A and C are incorrect. Ned's gesture is made without fuss and is thoughtful rather than a way of earning gratitude or admiration.

B is incorrect. There is no evidence that Ned found Kate's eyes mesmerising.

7   The brook is personified in the poem. It tells the reader about itself, its ways and its habits.

A is incorrect. It is the brook's speaking voice (constructed by the poet) that we hear.

C is incorrect. The natural world is described and spoken about but is not given a voice in the poem.

D is incorrect. Although at times the voice sounds like that of a man speaking, it differentiates itself from humankind by pointing out the different ways their lives end.

8   The movement of the brook is closely related to its surroundings. For example, it sallies forward quickly from its home and flows quickly down hills, it chatters and babbles its way over stones and it frets against its banks.

A is incorrect. The brook doesn't always move swiftly.

B is incorrect. The brook meanders very rarely.

C is incorrect. The brook often moves swiftly.

9   'Sharps' and 'trebles' are the names of high-pitched musical sounds. The words describe the nature of the sound the brook makes as it moves over stones and pebbles.

A is incorrect. The words refer to the sounds made by the brook, not the pebbles themselves.

B and D are incorrect. These options assume the sounds are made by things other than the brook, which is not the case. The use of the pronoun 'I', which represents the voice of the brook, makes it clear the noise is made by the brook's chatter.

10   The energy and liveliness of the brook are evident in the many verbs that denote activity (sparkle; bicker; slip; flow; join; go). Its journey is triumphant because it doesn't

end but continues for ever as a source of life to the world around it.

A is incorrect. The brook is joyous rather than sad or wistful.

C is incorrect. The poem presents the brook as a wonder of nature to be appreciated, not something to be laughed at.

D is incorrect. The brook doesn't set out to attack things in a belligerent way; rather it accommodates the natural world, asserting its power only when necessary for its survival.

11   The brook repeatedly asserts that, while people come and go, it lives on forever. From its perspective this gives it a definite advantage over humankind.

A is incorrect. The brook doesn't compare itself with nature.

B is incorrect. The brook sees itself as becoming part of the river rather than being superior or inferior to it.

D is incorrect. The brook speaks as though it has the power to absorb the lake and move it towards the river as part of itself.

12   In the previous sentence the author says merpeople are water-dwelling people represented in the legends of many different countries. This sentence points out the word mer in the name means sea, which relates to the fact they are water-dwelling: The word mer, or mere, is the old-English word for sea. The sentence that follows gives examples of other languages having similar words for sea.

13   In the previous sentence the author outlines the appearance of mermaids and mermen. This sentence gives information about where they live: These creatures live in the sea and are not able to survive on land. The sentence that follows describes a Selkie, who is a different kind of merperson because it can live on sea and on land.

14   In the previous sentence the author refers to a sea god, as a very early reference to a merperson. This sentence gives information about who recorded this information: Berossus, a priest and astronomer, wrote

about Ea, the early Babylonian sea god. The sentence that follows describes the features of Ea's appearance that characterise him as a merperson.

15 In the previous sentence the author is talking about unusual merpeople that occur in Chinese medieval stories. This sentence provides some details of how these figures behave: Some of these Chinese legendary figures live under water, like fish, but spend their time weaving and spinning silk. The sentence that follows adds some new information about what happens when these spinners cry.

16 In the previous sentence the author is talking about the growing belief in the existence of merpeople in the 18th century. This sentence explains that this was encouraged by reports from travellers who claimed to have seen actual merpeople: Many travellers reported seeing examples of them in captivity. The sentence that follows gives another example of sightings by fishermen, further adding support to the belief that merpeople exist.

17 In the previous sentence the author is talking about how people doubt the existence of merpeople. This sentence makes the point that even though people are sceptical, they are still often included in works of popular culture: Even so, merpeople are commonly included in literature, film and other types of popular culture. The sentence that follows gives examples from popular culture that include merpeople.

The unused sentence is E.

18 Information about the history of collecting and displaying miniature objects from previous centuries is provided in this text.

The other options are incorrect. No mention is made of previous centuries.

19 Three places within Australia are said to display oversized objects of local significance to attract tourists.

A and C are incorrect. These texts do not refer to particular places.

D is incorrect. Tsunamis are not an attraction.

20 The word large is used as a synonym for big to refer to the size of a wave that creates a tsunami.

A and B are incorrect. Although they repeatedly use the word big, they do not use synonyms for this word.

C is incorrect. This text is about tiny things.

21 The words 'GREAT BIG', for example, are printed in uppercase letters to make the words look larger and represent their meaning.

The other options are incorrect. In these texts the case of words is not changed to represent particular sizes or meanings.

22 The expression 'in the lap of the gods' means something is out of human control. It implies that the size and power of a tsunami is not controlled by humans.

The other options are incorrect. These texts do not address this implication.

23 Goldilocks, a little girl, is said to be about the same size as baby bear. Baby bear's chair is just the right size for her and baby bear is said to be 'no bigger than Goldilocks herself'.

A and D are incorrect. These texts do not include a girl and an animal.

C is incorrect. The animals mentioned in this text are of miniature size and so not similar in size to a child.

24 The request at the end of this text invites readers to send their opinions to a blog about whether or not constructing 'Big' objects as tourist attractions is a trend that will continue or die out.

The other options are incorrect. These texts do not include invitations to respond to a message.

25 The word miniature is defined and both children and adults are said to be attracted to miniature-sized objects and often collect them.

A and B are incorrect. These texts do not include definitions.

D is incorrect. Although this text includes the definition of a tsunami, these are not things adults or children are fond of.

SAMPLE Test 4

 Page 29

1 B 2 D 3 C 4 B 5 A 6 D 7 B 8 A 9 C
10 D 11 C 12 E 13 C 14 A 15 B 16 G
17 F 18 A 19 C 20 A 21 D 22 C 23 D
24 B 25 A

1 When Abel is exploring in his boat he feels much smaller and less significant than the vastness of the natural world around him; he is just a 'bubble on the sea', a dot in a seascape.

   A is incorrect. Although he is not yet adult sized, this is not why he feels small; even an adult would feel small in this situation.

   C is incorrect. He sees himself as being separate from the sea, as well as being different from it.

   D is incorrect. There is no evidence that looking through the glass of the waves magnifies the world he sees.

2 Abel's mother says they should do nothing to prevent Costello coming into the bay because she doesn't believe they have the legal right to do anything. She knows the water belongs to everyone and believes Costello has a right to be there that they can't legally challenge.

   A is incorrect. It is clear Abel's mother cares deeply about the bay and the damage Costello will probably cause there.

   B is incorrect. While she may hope Blueback would be able to look after himself, this is only a part of why she makes her decision to do nothing.

   C is incorrect. There is no evidence that fear of Costello harming Abel is behind her decision.

3 Abel and his mother disagree at times but they spend lots of time together, talk honestly to each other about what matters to them and care about the same things.

Therefore A and D are incorrect.

   B is incorrect. Although Abel and his mother are close, he remains independent and follows his own beliefs—as does she.

4 Costello is known for not respecting the environment and for stripping it of everything.

   A and C are incorrect. It is not just because Costello is an abalone diver who owns a jet boat that they fear him. It is because he greedily takes everything for himself.

   D is incorrect. Although Costello has a licence, it is the way he may take advantage of this licence that makes them afraid.

5 Abel is deeply concerned about Blueback's welfare. He swims with the big fish every chance he can and closely interacts with him in a way that is highly unusual.

   B is incorrect. The relationship between Abel and Blueback is the opposite of this; it is both very unusual and quite surprising.

   C is incorrect. Abel acts responsibly towards Blueback and cares a great deal about his fate.

   D is incorrect. There is no evidence that Abel's relationship with Blueback is either meaningless or destructive.

6 Abel was so shocked by his mother thinking about leaving their beloved home in the bay that he couldn't speak.

   A is incorrect. Abel would never come up with a solution that took them away from the bay or from Blueback.

   B is incorrect. Abel would not see the plan as a way to be 'saved'. He would never want to solve their problems by moving away.

   C is incorrect. While Abel finds it hard to believe his mother could suggest such a horrible plan, he trusts her and knows she loves the bay.

7 The poem is a conversation in the form of a dialogue between Father William and his son. The stanzas follow the pattern of the son

asking a question (stanzas 1, 3, 5 and 7) and the father replying to him (2, 4, 6 and 8).

A is incorrect. Their conversation does not tell a story.

C is incorrect. While various memories are mentioned, this is not the structure around which the poem is organised.

D is incorrect. There are two voices in the poem, not a single voice (a dialogue, not a monologue).

8 Although the son's questions are phrased in polite terms, they suggest his father is someone who spends his time foolishly and is grossly fat.

B and C are incorrect. Any praise the son seems to give is a way of highlighting his father's oddities.

D is incorrect. The son doesn't refer to any kind of forgetful behaviour connected with his father.

9 The father tells his son he was successful in his career in the law because he practised arguing with his wife before every case!

The other options are incorrect. The advice the father gives is not related to success in his career.

10 The differences between old and young are made fun of through a series of nonsensical questions and answers.

A is incorrect. The generation gap is not taken seriously and is treated in a comical, ridiculous way.

B is incorrect. There's no wisdom about the subject to be found in the poem.

C is incorrect. Sympathy is not extended to either character or the differences between them.

11 The father doesn't want to continue the conversation with his son so he breaks the pattern. Instead of beginning with 'In my youth ...', he says he's had enough.

A is incorrect. The father is firmly in control and has taken charge of the dialogue.

B is incorrect. The pattern of the son's question is unchanged from his previous questions.

D is incorrect. There is no evidence the poet wants to change the rhyme scheme and it remains the same as in previous stanzas (a/b/a/b).

12 In the previous sentence the author names the nation to which Bennelong belonged. This sentence tells where they lived at the time of the arrival of the British: When the British arrived in Australia in 1788, these people lived in the Port Jackson area. The sentence that follows tells what Bennelong did while growing up in that area.

13 In the previous sentence the author states how many sisters Bennelong had. This sentence reports a fact that was true of all his sisters: They married important men from nearby clans. The sentence that follows notes a reason why their new connections proved useful for Bennelong.

14 In the previous sentence the author states that Bennelong had a number of wives. This sentence tells us about his first wife: The first, whose name is not now known, died, probably from smallpox. The sentence that follows tells us about his second wife.

15 In the previous sentence the author refers to the two men Philip captured, naming the one who didn't escape as Bennelong. This sentence tells what happened to Bennelong after he was caught by Philip: He lived for a time in an upstairs room in Governor Philip's house, bringing his wife, Barangaroo, to visit. The sentence that follows explains that later he moved to a different home, one that Philip had built for him.

16 In the previous sentence the author describes some things Bennelong did in England when he visited. This sentence lists two more places he visited in London: He visited St Paul's Cathedral and the Tower of London. The sentence that follows explains why he left London.

17 In the previous sentence the author refers to a letter written by Bennelong to people he'd stayed with in England. This sentence tells what was in his letter: He thanked them for caring for him and also asked them to send him stockings and a handkerchief. The sentence that follows explains what makes this letter so special.

The unused sentence is D.

18 The male seahorse becomes pregnant and gives birth to its babies. There is no other species where this is the case.

B is incorrect. The birth process for kangaroos is not unique to its species.

C is incorrect. A star is not an animal.

D is incorrect. It is about the birth of a human baby, not an animal.

19 The explanation of how a star is born relies on numerous technical terms to describe the process. These terms include words such as 'galaxies', 'rotate', 'discs', 'core', 'hydrogen atoms', 'helium gas' and 'nuclear reaction'.

A and B are incorrect. Although they include some technical terms related to birth, they do not include as many terms as A.

D is incorrect. It does not include any technical terms about birth.

20 A giraffe is about 1.8 metres at birth—much larger than a jellybean.

B is incorrect. A baby kangaroo is about the size of a jellybean.

C is incorrect. It is not about the birth of an animal.

D is incorrect. It is about a human baby, not an animal baby.

21 A diary entry is not appropriate for inclusion in a science textbook as it includes personal opinions.

The other options are incorrect. They could be included in a science textbook about birth as they contain scientific facts about the birth of stars and of different animal species.

22 The birth of a star takes about a million years, a longer process than any of the others described.

A and B are incorrect. The birth processes described are much shorter than that of a star.

D is incorrect. The length of time of Billy's birth is not mentioned.

23 The new grandmother jokes with the mother about how quickly her new grandson will develop. Babies aren't able to talk or run around in the first weeks of their lives.

The other options are incorrect. They provide factual information, not personal exaggeration.

24 A newborn marsupial is kept safe in its mother's pouch.

A is incorrect. Neither newborn giraffes nor seahorses have places that keep them safe from the outside world while they are developing.

C and D are incorrect. They are not about baby animals.

25 The idea that male seahorses give birth rather than females in order to allow the females to be free to make more eggs is put forward as a possible scientific explanation or theory for this phenomenon.

The other options are incorrect. They do not refer to scientific theories.

SAMPLE Test 5 Page 35

1 C 2 A 3 B 4 A 5 D 6 A 7 D 8 A 9 A
10 B 11 D 12 B 13 A 14 D 15 C 16 F
17 G 18 B 19 C 20 D 21 A 22 B 23 A
24 C 25 D

1 Mrs Tulliver is embarrassed in front of her sisters about the wildness of Maggie's untidy hair. She is worried they will be critical of Maggie's appearance and it will reflect badly on her upbringing of Maggie.

A is incorrect. There is no evidence that Mrs Tulliver's voice is hoarse.

B is incorrect. As Tom is Maggie's brother, he would have heard her thoughts about Maggie's hair many times before.

D is incorrect. Although it is true Mrs Tulliver is ashamed of Maggie's appearance, this is not the reason she would choose to whisper a message to Maggie.

2 The aunts are shown in a very poor light: they make rude, personal comments about their niece and are bullying and bossy in their behaviour towards her.

B is incorrect. The reader is encouraged to feel critical of, rather than sympathetic towards, their behaviour.

C is incorrect. The author's judgement is implicit in her description of how the aunts talk and act.

D is incorrect. More than mild disapproval is implied. Their unkindness is revealed as a kind of torture that drives Maggie to behave in ways she shouldn't.

3 Maggie's first feelings are a sense of freedom being without the hair that caused her so much anxiety: 'as if she had emerged from a wood into the open plain'.

A is incorrect. She feels despairing soon after Tom cuts her hair but this is not her immediate feeling.

C is incorrect. Although she had imagined she would feel triumphant about escaping her family's comments about her hair, that is not what she feels immediately after Tom cuts her hair.

D is incorrect. Maggie does not feel horrified by what has been done.

4 As the consequences of cutting her hair sink in, Maggie begins to despair about what she has done. She realises she hasn't achieved what she was hoping for and now her chopped hair will be the centre of attention.

B is incorrect. Maggie's sense of being set free passes in a flash and is soon replaced with regrets.

C is incorrect. Maggie's hopes of feeling triumphant do not take place. She is too aware of the trouble she has caused herself.

D is incorrect. Although Maggie experiences regret and despair, she does not experience shock and is not filled with horror as the word 'horrified' suggests.

5 While Maggie's bursting into tears, stamping her foot and pushing at Tom may be understandable given the degree of her distress, it is certainly quick tempered, angry behaviour. Tom's use of the word 'spitfire' in relation to this behaviour may be a little extreme but is reasonably accurate.

The other options are incorrect. They all imply there is no justification for Tom's choice of the word 'spitfire' to describe her behaviour.

6 The author shows Maggie in a sympathetic light in this paragraph. She calls her 'poor Maggie' and underlines how frequently and painfully her 'small soul' has had to suffer during her childhood. She is shown to be passionate and impulsive but not intentionally cruel or unkind.

B is incorrect. The emphasis is less on Maggie's foolishness than on the torment she suffers.

C is incorrect. Although Tom behaves rather callously in leaving Maggie behind and hurrying downstairs to dinner, this is another detail that arouses sympathy for Maggie.

D is incorrect. The paragraph is not about Maggie's ingratitude to her family.

7 The speaker is imagining 'quiet' as a person in a game of hide and seek. She is the one doing the seeking and 'quiet' is what she wants to find.

A is incorrect because none of the speaker's friends are mentioned.

B and C are incorrect because the forest and the sea are places where she searches, not who/what she searches for.

8   The speaker finds the forest full of jarring, overwhelming sounds. The two hard, grating 'c' sounds, used with an 'a' between to suggest something unpleasant—'cac'—echo the racket of sound she wants to escape.

The other options are incorrect. The 'c' sounds in the word 'cacophony' are harsh, not melodious, gentle or spooky.

9   When the speaker dismisses the forest as a place to find 'quiet', her tone is frustrated and disappointed. She has failed to find what she wanted there.

B and D are incorrect. The expression, 'so much for ...' is spoken with too much confidence to convey anxiety or bewilderment.

C is incorrect. Although there may be some annoyance in her tone, she is in control of her emotions and does not convey fury.

10 The rhythm of the two evenly repeated syllables (non-stop, non-stop) echoes the beat of the waves as it relentlessly slaps the seaweed on to the sand.

A is incorrect. The 'squarking' of the seagulls is not described as having this particular rhythm.

C is incorrect. The zig-zagging movements of the sea things suggest a counter rhythm to the regular beat of the waves coming to shore.

D is incorrect. The trumpeting of the sea suggests a long trumpet blast of sound rather than a regular beat.

11 The speaker is caught by surprise when 'quiet' finds her. She is 'tagged', as in a game of hide and seek and she finds 'quiet' in a place where she least expected it to be: hidden inside herself.

A is incorrect. Her searches are unsuccessful.

B is incorrect. It is not who takes turns that determines how 'quiet' is found.

C is incorrect. 'Quiet' has stayed well hidden inside her; she is not the one who is well hidden.

12 In the previous sentence the author states that UFOs definitely exist. This sentence confirms that we know this because people report seeing them: People regularly see objects flying in the atmosphere that are unable to be identified. The sentence that follows makes suggestions about possible explanations for what they are seeing.

13 In the previous sentence the author says there is no proof that UFOs are extra-terrestrial. This sentence defines the meaning of extra-terrestrial: That is, that they come from outside the earth's atmosphere. The sentence that follows adds there is also lack of proof that extra-terrestrial objects are piloted by aliens!

14 In the previous sentence the author says governments treat UFOs as a phenomenon that must be treated seriously. This sentence confirms their serious attitude by stating they record what they learn about the sightings: They keep careful records of sightings on file. The sentence that follows states that while many of these sightings prove to be fake, others are still unexplained.

15 In the previous sentence the author asks if there might be universes unknown to humans. This sentence gives an answer to this question: Some scientists claim it is clear that earth is not the only inhabited planet. The sentence that follows gives more detail about the nature of life on these planets that scientists think could exist.

16 In the previous sentence the author refers to a wave of sightings in Belgium. This sentence tells when this wave took place: These sightings lasted from 1989 to 1990. The sentence that follows lists the numbers who saw the UFO on the night when sightings peaked.

17 In the previous sentence the author refers to a personal claim related to an attempted abduction. This sentence names the couple who made the claim: It was reported by an American couple, Barney and Betty Hill. The sentence that follows reports that

investigators into their claims are still baffled by the evidence they provided.

The unused sentence is E.

18 The destruction of the Twin Towers in 2001 killed many people and very few in the vicinity survived the impact.

A is incorrect. This text is about a shipwrecked man with no survivors mentioned.

C is incorrect. No single event is described in this text.

D is incorrect. Although the family's capsized boat led to terrible disaster, it was an accident rather than a hostile event.

19 Both the camel and the camel spider survive well in a desert environment.

The other options are incorrect. These texts are not about unrelated animals.

20 It is explained that by following their parents' instructions and using the survival skills they had been taught, the children managed to survive.

The other options are incorrect. These texts do not include explanations about children who survive an accident.

21 Robinson Crusoe is the sole survivor from a shipwreck. The ways he sets about rebuilding his life on the island are described in some detail.

B is incorrect. Although it is about an individual tree, it is saved by others, not itself.

C and D are incorrect. These texts are not about individuals.

22 Those people who rescued the Callery Pear Tree saved its life so it could be replanted and bloom again. The replanted tree, at the Memorial at New York's World Trade Centre, is a symbol of hope and resilience for humans, as are the tree's seeds when they are sent to suffering communities.

A is incorrect. This text tells the story of an individual taking action to aid his own survival.

C is incorrect. This text refers to ways in which animal behaviour can aid their survival.

D is incorrect. This text shows how the natural world can both help and hinder human survival. It is also not about how humans help the natural world.

23 The narrator, Robinson Crusoe, lists the many and varied hardships he faces in the second paragraph.

The other options are incorrect. Although hardships are mentioned in these texts, they are not listed together.

24 Cockroaches are described as having adapted to living almost anywhere.

The other options are incorrect. The people and animals referred to in these texts are not said to survive in all environments.

25 Torres Strait Islander peoples view survival skills as being so important in their community that they teach them to children from a very young age.

The other options are incorrect. These texts are not about how a particular culture views survival skills.

SAMPLE Test 6 Page 41

1 B 2 C 3 D 4 A 5 B 6 A 7 C 8 A 9 B
10 D 11 C 12 G 13 C 14 A 15 B 16 F
17 D 18 C 19 A 20 B 21 D 22 A 23 D
24 D 25 C

1 The children can hear cannon fire 'again' so we know there is a war going on around them. They are keeping themselves hidden in a farmhouse that seems to have been abandoned by its owners.

A is incorrect. Although it is true they are by themselves in a farmhouse, they are taking shelter there rather than living there permanently.

C is incorrect. While the barn looks like a gingerbread house from the window of the farmhouse, they are not playing inside it.

D is incorrect. There is no-one else in the farmhouse with them. They only have photos of Oma and Opa.

2 The story is told in the first person by a narrator who is Otto's older sister. She takes care of Otto and Mia. You can work out her name is Liesl as she is in the photo with Otto and Mia.

A is incorrect. The author has created a character, Otto's older sister, to tell the story from her point of view.

B is incorrect. What Otto does and says is reported by the narrator. He does not tell the reader what happens.

D is incorrect. Otto does not have an older brother. He only jokes that he would have one if his sister dressed up in boy's clothes.

3 You can work out from the text that the children have been travelling through a war-torn landscape for some time, without access to a place to wash. They have become filthy and their clothes are dirty and ragged.

A is incorrect. They love having a bath when they get the chance.

B is incorrect. Although it is very cold, they are able to heat the water for their bath in the empty farmhouse.

C is incorrect. You can work out the war has separated the children from their parents so their parents cannot care for them.

4 Otto gets 'lost in the moment' and feels things intensely. His expressions reveal his strong feelings: his face lights up, he grins, he teases, he scrunches his nose, he becomes concerned, all in a short space of time.

B and C are incorrect. Otto is impulsive rather than cool-headed or sensible.

D is incorrect. Otto clearly cares about his sisters and treats them with affection.

5 The narrator blushes because she has just lied to Otto by saying they haven't stolen the clothes, just borrowed them. His question makes her confront the truth of the situation which she was trying not to face.

A is incorrect. She knows Otto does not want to steal the clothes even though he wants to keep them.

C is incorrect. While it is true the narrator is embarrassed, it is not because of her choice of a jumper; it is because they are all stealing clothes that aren't theirs.

D is incorrect. She is glad Otto is having fun. Her blushing is directly associated with being caught out in a lie, however well-meant her words.

6 The narrator may technically have committed the 'crimes' she accuses herself of, but she is not responsible for them in the context in which they have happened. She does not deserve the condemnation she piles on herself.

B is incorrect. Her assessment of her actions is quite unfair given that she is a victim of an ongoing war.

C is incorrect. The story makes clear she is a worthy, loving person who values truth and goodness.

D is incorrect. The list of crimes the narrator accuses herself of comes as an unexpected shock even though the reader knows she has in fact done these things.

7 The natural world is tamed at every turn into places that are characterised by order for humans to enjoy. Its beauty is gentle and non-threatening.

A is incorrect. This world is not chaotic or disorganized as every view of it is pleasantly arranged.

B is incorrect. Although soft colours are referred to and are in keeping with its gentle nature, they are not its most characteristic component.

D is incorrect. While shadow is referred to, it is part of a larger pattern of orderliness.

8 It is the dramatic contrasts of the world of stanza two—droughts and floods, beauty and terror—that reveal why the speaker finds her country so wonderfully full of energy and life.

B is incorrect. The opposite of suffering is just as much a part of this world.

C is incorrect. While there is beauty there is also pain and suffering.

D is incorrect. While wide open spaces are celebrated, what the poet sees as characterising this land are the contrasts within that space.

9   When the land itself is burnt by the sun, the summer is fiercely hot.

A is incorrect. It is the country that is sunburnt, not the people.

C is incorrect. There is no specific reference to climate change in the poem.

D is incorrect. While the land is burnt by the sun, it is not implied that it is on fire.

10 The speaker accepts both the terror and beauty of this country and wants to embrace it all, exactly as it is.

A is incorrect. Although the speaker accepts the terror, she goes further than this by wanting to embrace everything the country offers, whether good or bad.

B and C are incorrect. There is no evidence the speaker either rejects or ignores the terror that is part of her country.

11 The feelings the speaker describes that she has for her country are intense and passionate. She loves everything about it—even the things that are destructive and painful. It is the whole of it—its energy, drama and wonder—that she embraces.

A and B are incorrect. Her feelings go beyond anything as moderate as warm affection (A) or as mild as supportiveness (B).

D is incorrect. While the speaker is no doubt loyal and devoted to her country, the feelings she expresses in this poem go beyond this to a wilder passion at the 'core' of her heart: an intense love for everything about her country.

12 In the previous sentence the author defines a kite as something which has a light frame covered with material. This sentence adds the

further detail that the frame may have a tail attached: The frame often has a tail to stabilise it. The sentence that follows explains there is also a string attached to the frame to enable it to be flown.

13 In the previous sentence the author refers to the history of kites. This sentence tells where that history began: The earliest known examples are from Asia from some two and three thousand years ago. The sentence that follows explains knowledge about this history is based on records from ancient Asian cultures.

14 In the previous sentence the author explains it is thought Marco Polo introduced the idea of kites to Europeans. This sentence explains how he was able to learn about kites when in China: He journeyed there on the Silk Road, a trade route joining East and West, towards the end of the 13th century. The sentence that follows explains the kind of information he passed on about kites when he returned to Europe.

15 In the previous sentence the author points out that some cultures are known for using kites in particular ways. This sentence explains that Chinese people are known for using kites as part of their war strategies: Chinese armies, for example, have used them as instruments of warfare in strategies to defeat their enemies. The sentence that follows provides an example of a particular strategy a Chinese General used.

16 In the previous sentence the author states that kites have been useful in scientific experiments in various countries. This sentence lists some of the ways they have been used for these purposes: Measuring distances, calculating wind readings and assisting with experiments related to flight are examples. The sentence that follows explains another form of use for kites in a scientific field.

17 In the previous sentence the author refers to a use for kites that is common across cultures. This sentence describes another popular

cross-cultural use: They provide entertainment for audiences of young and old at kite festivals to celebrate cultural or spiritual events. The sentence that follows adds yet another example: that of children getting pleasure from kite flying wherever they are placed in the world.

The unused sentence is E.

18 The author gives Ming the Mollusc its own voice. Using the first person, Ming talks about its previous life and how it ended up as a ghost!

The other options are incorrect. None of these texts is about a talking marine creature.

19 The crew used three mechanical sharks when making the film.

The other options are incorrect. The marine animals in these texts are not artificial or mechanically made.

20 You can work out that the Gubbi Gubbi people of Queensland are a First Nations Australian language group who viewed the lungfish as sacred.

The other options are incorrect. First Australian attitudes are not referred to in these texts.

21 The bottlenose dolphin's whistling is like a thumbprint in that no two whistling patterns are alike. They are used as a means of identifying individuals, just as thumbprints are.

The other options are incorrect. The features described in these texts are not unique in the same way as a thumbprint.

22 It is suggested that attitudes towards killing sharks have shifted from the more aggressive attitudes of the seventies to today where there is more awareness of their importance in the ecosystem.

B is incorrect. It is not stated in this text what current attitudes are in relation to the eating of, or need for conserving, lungfish.

C and D are incorrect, These texts do not deal with changing attitudes towards ecological awareness.

23 The importance of sound in the lives of dolphins and whales is the focus of this text.

The other options are incorrect. The focus of these texts is not on the role of a particular sense in the lives of marine creatures.

24 Several species of marine animals are referred to but no creatures are humanised with a personal name

A is incorrect. A lungfish named Methuselah is a character mentioned in this text.

B is incorrect. Mechanical sharks nicknamed Bruce are characters mentioned in this text.

C is incorrect. Ming the Mollusc is a character mentioned.

25 This text refers to scientists who mistakenly killed a 507-year-old mollusc when trying to measure its age.

The other options are incorrect. There is no mention in these texts of mistakes made by scientists when carrying out their research.

SAMPLE Test 7 Page 48

1 B 2 C 3 D 4 C 5 A 6 D 7 C 8 C 9 B
10 C 11 D 12 B 13 F 14 A 15 C 16 E
17 D 18 A 19 D 20 B 21 C 22 B 23 A
24 D 25 C

1 The story is about a time when the world is new and the Animals are beginning to work for Man. This means it is near the time when the world began.

A and D are incorrect. This text is set inside time near the beginning of the world's creation, not outside.

C is incorrect. The story takes place near the beginning of the world, so not near its ending.

2 The Camel's laziness is extremely irritating for everyone: it causes trouble for Man, for the other Animals and for the Djinn.

A and B are incorrect. Although the Camel is vain and spends time gazing at its reflection

(A) and replies rudely to everyone (B), these qualities are less irritating than its laziness.

D is incorrect. The Camel does not lie (it just says 'Humph') and it doesn't act in a deceptive way.

3 When the Camel refuses to work, the Man has to make the other Animals do its work as well as their own.

A is incorrect. The Camel's laziness makes the Man cross with the Camel, not with the other Animals.

B and C are incorrect. There is no evidence the Animals begin to copy the Camel nor that they summon the Djinn. The Djinn comes of his own accord.

4 The Djinn knows the Camel cannot resist saying 'Humph', especially when work is mentioned. He warns the camel not to say that word again, as there will be consequences, and then entices him to say it by telling him he wants him to work.

A is incorrect. The Djinn speaks sternly and politely to the Camel, not rudely.

B is incorrect. Although the Djinn uses magic in various ways in the story, such as adding a hump to the Camel's back, he uses trickery rather than magic to make the Camel trap itself.

D is incorrect. The Djinn does not laugh at the Camel to make it do what he wants it to do.

5 The Djinn's plan is very clever because it turns the Camel's word ('Humph') into an actual hump on its back. This makes it possible for it to work for three days at a time without eating, solving everyone's problems.

B is incorrect. The Djinn's plan solves everyone's problems and doesn't create any new ones.

C is incorrect. The Djinn's plan is a creative and unusual solution.

D is incorrect. The Djinn's plan is highly practical and successful.

6 The Djinn's magic transforms the camel by giving him a hump that stores his food so he can work for three days at a time without eating.

A is incorrect. It is stated that even though the Camel begins to work, it never learns how to behave.

B is incorrect. There is no evidence to suggest the Camel becomes more respectful of the other Animals.

C is incorrect. While it is said the Camel still doesn't behave well, it is not suggested that it grows more disobedient than it was before.

7 The main thing that makes Macavity a 'Mystery Cat' is his ability to vanish from the scene of any crime he has committed.

The other options are incorrect. While Macavity likes to break the law, could be called a criminal (he steals, for example) and pretends to be asleep when he is awake, these qualities are not what give him the reputation of being a 'Mystery Cat'.

8 The word 'looted' suggests a particularly nasty form of stealing as it generally takes place in a time of war or unrest. The poet is building Macavity's reputation as a master criminal.

A is incorrect. No-one is in danger or made to feel afraid by Macavity's actions.

B is incorrect. By labelling Macavity's thefts as looting, the poet implies it is a crime and there is nothing 'reasonable' about his behaviour.

D is incorrect. Although Macavity's behaviour is naughty, the word 'looted' makes it seem very much worse than this.

9 Macavity's crimes include stealing milk, food and other objects, fighting off Pekes (Pekingese dogs), breaking glass and garden trellises, and 'shredding' papers on a desk. These are all things many cats do in their day-to-day lives but the poet presents them as though they are examples of theft, murder, violent destruction and espionage!

A and C are incorrect. The poet presents the crimes as worse than they are, not trivial (A) or unimportant (C).

D is incorrect. The word 'fiend' suggests behaviour that is evil and not just the naughtiness of a cat.

10 The poet is in awe of Macavity's trickery and accomplishments. This is not to say he approves of what he does, but he repeatedly expresses wonder at how he escapes detection: '*Macavity's not there!*'

The other options are incorrect. Although the poet judges Macavity's crimes as worthy of strong disapproval, the dominant tone he adopts when telling us about them is awe or wonder (almost admiration!).

11 In the last stanza it is revealed that Macavity has an army of helpers he controls as efficiently as Napoleon controlled his troops. These agents do his bidding and, it is implied, would provide Macavity with an alibi if needed.

A is incorrect. There is no evidence that Macavity changes his shape when he wants to disappear (although the poet does wonder if Macavity is an evil spirit who has taken the form of a cat: 'a fiend in feline form').

B is incorrect. Some of the 'agents' who help him are identified in the poem: '(I might mention Mungojerrie, I might mention Griddlebone)'.

C is incorrect. Although Macavity manages to keep his whereabouts secret, this does not explain how he always has an alibi.

12 In the previous sentence the author asks a question about why men have different hairstyles at different times. This sentence offers an explanation: It is often related to following a fashion that is in vogue. The sentence that follows offers other possible explanations to answer this question.

13 In the previous sentence the author states that braiding of hair in China was a response to a spiritual belief. This sentence gives more detail about that belief: The cutting of hair was frowned on as it was viewed as a gift from ancestors. The sentence that follows provides an example of Chinese people who followed this practice.

14 In the previous sentence the author refers to the bowl cut being a common style in Europe in the Middle Ages. This sentence tells what the style looks like: This style looked as if a bowl had been placed on the head and then scissors used to cut around its shape. The sentence that follows points out that often it was cut in exactly that way!

15 In the previous sentence the author states that military needs often dictate men's hairstyles. This sentence explains how this is true of the Samurai: From as long ago as the ninth century, Samurai warriors have had their hair cut in a style designed to stabilise their helmets during battle. The sentence that follows gives details of the style they used to achieve this goal.

16 In the previous sentence the author has noted that modern armies favour short hair for men. This sentence explains why this is so: This is because short hair is easily managed and easy to keep clean and well-groomed. The sentence that follows gives an example of a style of short hair used in United States armies.

17 In the previous sentence the author states that modern Australian men choose a variety of hairstyles. This sentence tells you where you can view some of these: If you visit your local mall, you'll see men with part shaving and undercutting styles. The sentence that follows lists more of the styles you are likely to see there.

The unused sentence is G.

18 The loss of available wetland areas, which are essential resting and feeding places for Bar-tailed Godwits on their return journeys to the northern hemisphere, would be of great concern to conservationists.

The other options are incorrect. They don't deal with issues about species that would concern conservationists.

19 The animals who travel incredible distances in difficult circumstances are all inspired by a longing to return to the homes they have been removed from.

A is incorrect. Although the birds' journeys represent, in a sense, a longing for 'home', they are more about reaching destinations that meet their needs related to, for example, resources and climate.

B is incorrect. Jessica Watson went on a single journey that was inspired by a dream or ambition to sail around the world, not by a longing to be home.

C is incorrect. Luis Soriano's journeys on his donkeys are inspired by wanting to reach remote areas.

20 Jessica's blog, an online web log that records a person's activities, thoughts and so on, is described as her way of communicating with those interested in her journey.

The other options are incorrect. They do not refer to forms of communication related to the internet.

21 Luis Soriano's work with his travelling library has had a wide-reaching effect on helping children in his community and has led to the city having its own library.

A is incorrect. This text is about animal, not human, communities.

B is incorrect. Although Jessica Watson's achievement in completing her journey around the world inspired admiration, it did not contribute directly to bettering her community.

D is incorrect. The animal journeys described have an effect on individuals or families rather than communities.

22 It was the book Jessica's mother read to her that inspired her dream of sailing around the world.

A and D are incorrect. None of these journeys are inspired by a book.

C is incorrect. Although it is implied that Luis Soriano's journeys would have been inspired by his love of books, it is not said he ever listened to a particular book that was inspirational to him.

23 Books are not mentioned in this text.

B is incorrect. One book is named.

C is incorrect. Books are a focus of this text.

D is incorrect. Several books and their authors are named.

24 The scene when Lassie finds her way home after a long, difficult journey and is reunited with her owner, Jo, is described as 'tear-jerking': an emotional response to an emotional scene.

A is incorrect. The emotional impact of the birds' journeys is not addressed.

B is incorrect. The reaction to Jessica's achievement is excitement and wonder at her success, not its emotional impact on those involved.

C is incorrect. Hundreds of journeys were involved, not a single journey.

25 Luis and his donkeys work together to help children in remote areas of their community. The journeys are arduous and dangerous and require a special kind of co-operation between man and beast.

A is incorrect. The animals in this text make their journeys on their own initiative.

B is incorrect. Animals are not referred to in this text.

D is incorrect. Humans are not referred to in this text.

SAMPLE Test 8   Page 56

1 C 2 B 3 C 4 A 5 B 6 D 7 C 8 D 9 B
10 B 11 A 12 C 13 E 14 A 15 B 16 G
17 F 18 C 19 A 20 B 21 B 22 D 23 C
24 A 25 D

1   The story is a narrative about the adventures of three boys who survive a shipwreck.

A is incorrect. The text is not about disasters created by scientific and technological discoveries or inventions of the future.

B is incorrect. The text is not about people who make contact with witches, giants or other supernatural agents.

D is incorrect. The text does not use animal characters to convey a moral lesson.

2   The opening is full of the narrator's excited, happy anticipation of a sea voyage while the ending is much more subdued and uncertain.

A is incorrect. There is nothing similar in the moods of the opening and ending of the story.

C is incorrect. The opposite is true: nothing at all dramatic occurs in the opening.

D is incorrect. Although in the opening the narrator describes the scene as 'a delightful dream', the mood is of his delight and joy and is not at all dreamlike.

3   The sailor who hoists the anchor on board refers to it as though it were a female.

A is incorrect. Although a ship is traditionally referred to as female, it is the anchor of the ship that is referred to as a 'lass' here.

B and D are incorrect. None of the people referred to in the text are female.

4   Once the rudder is torn off, the ship can no longer be steered or controlled and can easily be smashed onto the rocks by the huge waves.

B is incorrect. Being lashed to the wheel is no help once the rudder has been torn off.

C is incorrect. While being blown off course is extremely dangerous, having their rudder smashed while being near the rocks is more so.

D is incorrect. While the loss of the masts makes it dangerous for the sailors, this is not as dangerous as having no rudder.

5   Without Jack's plan, the three young friends would have ended up with the sailors lost at sea from the small boat.

A is incorrect. While Peterkin's kindness may have helped the narrator, without Jack's plan they wouldn't have made it to the shore.

C is incorrect. While the narrator's strength may have helped him to hang on to the oar, without Jack's plan he would not have had that option.

D is incorrect. Although the wild waves washed the oar to a place where the friends could hold onto it, without Jack's plan they wouldn't have been in a position to use it.

6   It is implied the sailors would have drowned after being flung from their small boat into the wild seas.

A and B are incorrect. These are statements of fact about events that took place, not what the rest of the sailors' fates might have been.

C is incorrect. It was the three friends who escaped the shipwreck by reaching an island, not the rest of the sailors.

7   The narrator's name was easy on the ear in Poland. Its sounds didn't jar or stand out but flowed sweetly.

A is incorrect. The simile emphasises the sweet, flowing sounds of his name and doesn't refer to whether or not it was commented upon.

B is incorrect. Although it may have been a popular name, the narrator does not use the simile of snow melting to imply its popularity.

D is incorrect. There is no reference to the way it was spelt.

8   The narrator thinks his Polish name sounds ugly when he is with people who don't speak Polish. The sounds are distorted and clatter off their tongues, causing him embarrassment.

A and C are incorrect. There is no evidence that he forgets his Polish name (A) or that he wishes he was back there (C).

B is incorrect. We are only given one example of when he calls himself Jim.

9 The narrator creates a threatening atmosphere at the coffee shop by describing the baristas as aggressive and warlike and by making the person selling the coffee seem like an inquisitor who is preparing a record about him for judgement day.

A and D are incorrect. There is nothing the narrator finds cheerful or relaxing about being at the local coffee shop on this occasion.

C is incorrect. While the narrator certainly finds the atmosphere uncomfortable, he makes it seem much more intimidating than this.

10 The narrator lies by pretending his name is Jim. He doesn't want to use his real name because he knows it will sound ugly and unattractive in this context.

The other options are incorrect. He knows his name (A), he does bite his tongue (C) and his comment about his name 'pouring' through the ears of Polish people is not a lie but a metaphor for how it sounded (D).

11 The moment of giving a false name is a tense moment for the narrator. It takes courage in the intimidating atmosphere of the coffee shop and he involuntarily bites his tongue as he tells his 'lie'.

B is incorrect. Although he may feel some pride in what he does, uneasiness about lying is uppermost.

C is incorrect. Although fear of ridicule may have caused him to lie, the situation is not one of terror.

D is incorrect. While he may have appeared confident when he stared into the eyes of the Recording Angel, inwardly he was feeling quite nervous and unsettled.

12 In the previous sentence the author reports that Pretzel, a green turtle hatchling, was washed ashore by floods. This sentence names the beach where he landed: He ended up at New Brighton Beach on the north coast of New South Wales. The sentence that follows explains what happened to him after

this: he was rescued and taken into care at a Wildlife hospital.

13 In the previous sentence the author refers to a new problem for Pretzel. This sentence describes this new problem: He had suffered being swept from his home but now an X-ray showed he had a blockage in his colon. The sentence that follows explains what had caused this new problem.

14 In the previous sentence the author says there was concern about the seawater being used for the rescued sea creatures. This sentence explains what that concern was: The impact of the floods on the seawater had affected its quality. The sentence that follows explains how this led to the sea creatures being moved to the Gold Coast where the seawater was of better quality.

15 In the previous sentence the author says Pretzel still had a piece of the plastic in his body. This sentence points out Pretzel was in luck as the scientist found a way to remove it: Fortunately the scientist was able to remove this by hand using tweezers. The sentence that follows jokes that Pretzel had used up another of his lives.

16 In the previous sentence the author states that scientists are horrified by the damage caused by plastics to marine life. This sentence explains why this is so: They harm internal organs as they can't be digested and this causes numerous deaths. The sentence that follows says how this problem has been made even worse by floods.

17 In the previous sentence the author says how Mr James Weiss comments on the problem of plastics in our oceans. This sentence refers to information about a possible partial solution to this problem: He sees the international agreement formed to take action to reduce plastic waste across the world as a hopeful sign. The sentence that follows warns that individuals also must bear responsibility for helping to solve the problem of plastic pollution.

The unused sentence is D.

18 What happens to Captain Briggs is not explained as none of them were ever seen or heard of again.

   A and D are incorrect. There are no named people included in these texts.

   B is incorrect. We are told that Dean Harrison is still working on solving the mystery of the Yowie.

19 Research attempting to solve the mystery of why sea lions have begun to return to New Zealand is not mentioned in this text.

   The other options are incorrect. They all refer to research that has been undertaken to solve their mysteries.

20 The continents of Australia and North America report many sightings of large hairy creatures that sound similar but which remain unidentified.

   The other options are incorrect. They do not compare mysteries from different continents.

21 Dean Harrison has made progress with his ambition to establish the existence of the Yowie and believes he is close to doing so.

   A and D are incorrect. Individuals are not named in these texts.

   C is incorrect. The individual named, Captain Briggs, disappeared long ago from the scene of the mystery.

22 It is suggested that rails have lost their ability to fly because, over time, flying has become unnecessary for them.

   The other options are incorrect. The mysteries they describe are not caused by a change in characteristics of a species.

23 Early theories to explain the abandonment of the *Mary Celeste* included the possibility of an explosion. Recent research using modern technologies demonstrates how that could have happened without damaging the ship.

   A is incorrect. Neither technologies nor theories about the mystery are included.

B is incorrect. Although recent technologies are being used to try to establish the existence of the Yowie, it is not about theories that aim to explain its existence.

   D is incorrect. Recent technologies are used to establish a new theory that explains the mystery, not to support an earlier theory.

24 The mystery of why sea lions have returned to New Zealand has not been solved but conservationists are keen to take the opportunity of a second chance so they can rebuild their populations.

   The other options are incorrect. They do not refer to conservationists.

25 The solution offered to the mystery of how rails that can't fly reached Inaccessible Island is very convincing and no other explanation seems possible.

   A is incorrect. No solution to the mystery is supplied.

   B is incorrect. Although Dean Harrison's photographic work sounds as if it might turn out to be evidence of strange creatures' existence, it is unlikely this will explain all the sightings over time and in different places of similar creatures.

   C is incorrect. Although the solution convincingly explains part of what may have happened, it leaves unanswered questions: why did the people leave when they did if their boat was undamaged and what happened to them?

SAMPLE Test 9   Page 62

1 C 2 D 3 B 4 B 5 D 6 C 7 B 8 A 9 D
10 B 11 C 12 B 13 F 14 A 15 D 16 E
17 G 18 A 19 D 20 C 21 A 22 B 23 C
24 D 25 B

1 Lenny looks after Lady by feeding her and keeping her safe. She hides her from her mother because she guesses she would not allow Lenny to keep her.

   A is incorrect. Lenny clearly cares about Lady and feels connected to her.

B is incorrect. Although Lenny is very careful of Lady, there is no evidence she is fussy or over particular.

D is incorrect. Although it may be unkind and heartless to keep a ladybug in a jar, Lenny doesn't realise this. She thinks Lady is happy.

2 Timothy is Davey's imaginary golden eagle.

A is incorrect. The pigeons are named Roger, Martin and Frank.

B is incorrect. The ladybug in the story is named Lady.

C is incorrect. Davey doesn't have a brother in the story.

3 Lenny and Davey make up imaginary running-away stories together. Running away to Canada and reaching Great Bear Lake is a favourite story of theirs.

A is incorrect. Canada is referred to as a place they want to visit, not the place where they live.

C is incorrect. We are not told where the pigeons like to visit.

D is incorrect. There is no evidence the children have actually visited Canada. What they know about it, they have learned from an encyclopedia article.

4 Lenny does not have an imaginary friend, although Davey does, which makes this statement false.

A is incorrect. We know both Lenny and Davey love learning about things through reading an encyclopedia.

C is incorrect. Both Lenny and Davey are keenly interested in animals, ladybugs and pigeons in particular.

D is incorrect. Lenny acts kindly towards Davey by making up stories with him and not making fun of his behaviour. Davey is kind to Lenny by not giving away her secret to his mother.

5 Their imaginary running-away story is interrupted when Lenny thinks of their mother discovering what they had done. The shock of this thought jolts them back to the reality of what they were planning to do.

A is incorrect. Although Lenny describes the balloon snagging on a powerline, this is just another imaginary event—a way of mentally bringing their dream to an end.

B is incorrect. There is no evidence Lenny was unable to imagine the next step of their journey.

C is incorrect. Davey's comment about the bathroom came earlier and, although Lenny says his words could ruin their fantasy, this is not the thought that causes the jolt which ends it.

6 Lenny's words recognise their imaginings are just talk but she thinks of them as a beginning rather than an ending. This makes her words hopeful rather than despairing about what might happen.

A is incorrect. Her words are not as pessimistic as this.

B is incorrect. Lenny and Davey share a similar view of the world that tends to be positive and hopeful.

D is incorrect. There is no evidence Lenny's words refer specifically to Davey.

7 The paths 'diverged' in the sense that they were separate from each other and offered the speaker a choice of which to take.

A and C are incorrect. It is the separateness of the paths that leads to the choice; they are not united or merged together.

D is incorrect. Although the end of the paths is out of sight, they don't literally vanish.

8 The speaker's tone, as he talks about his moment of choice, is relaxed and casual. It is as if he is speaking to himself, recollecting a particular moment, in a personal, conversational way.

B and C are incorrect. The speaker accepts the idea that once the choice is made, it is not useful to worry about 'what if …'.

D is incorrect. The speaker's tone is friendly and confiding rather than pompous and self-important.

9 The speaker acknowledges there was very little difference between the paths, yet at the time he thought he was choosing the path that looked less travelled.

A is incorrect. He says he made a conscious, not a random, choice.

B is incorrect. He says both paths were without evidence of recent tracks through their black leaves.

C is incorrect. The speaker says there was a particular reason he made his choice: it looked less travelled.

10 The speaker knows 'how way leads on to way' from his experience of life. Once you are on a path you are led to new choices that take you forward.

A is incorrect. He imagines himself when he is old but that time has not yet come.

C and D are incorrect. He doesn't know whether or not it would be a waste of time or a mistake; he just knows it is unlikely he would ever come back because he knows you get caught up in the journey you have chosen.

11 The two paths represent different choices or opportunities in life. When you follow one, you are taken on a journey that means you have had to leave the chances represented by the other path behind.

A is incorrect. As far as the speaker can see at the time of making the choice, the paths look very similar. They may represent different, but not necessarily opposing, choices.

B is incorrect. The roads stand for the choices to be made and do not represent attitudes towards change.

D is incorrect. The roads both show a way ahead. They both lead to a future but a different future from each other.

12 In the previous sentence the author says what a fairy ring looks like. This sentence tells how it is usually formed: The ring is usually formed by mushrooms that grow in a circular pattern. The sentence that follows tells of another way fairy rings can be formed.

13 In the previous sentence the author explains how a mushroom spore is responsible for the growth of a fairy ring. This sentence explains what the mushroom spore does: It builds a network of tubular threads underground in a circular shape. The sentence that follows explains that the result is a circle of mushroom caps.

14 In the previous sentence the author says the cause of spinifex grass rings in the Australian outback is still uncertain. This sentence suggests a possible explanation: A recent scientific explanation is the possibility that microbes eat away at the older parts of the spinifex. The sentence that follows tells us this might have led to the rings being formed.

15 In the previous sentence the author tells of a belief some hold about the nature of fairy rings. This sentence refers to another belief that is held about fairy rings: Others assume that the ring is a sign of an underground fairy village. The sentence that follows describes a third belief about the nature of fairy rings.

16 In the previous sentence the author points out it is thought that fairy rings can have their dangers. This sentence explains what some believe that danger to be: If you step inside, it is thought, you may be in danger of becoming instantly invisible. The sentence that follows gives another view about what happens if you step inside a fairy ring.

17 In the previous sentence the author tells what Dutch people think about fairy rings and their dangers. This sentence compares this belief with the view of the Welsh: In contrast, the Welsh see the rings as signs of the fertile soil that is nearby. The sentence that follows tells what the Welsh do as a result of their belief.

The unused sentence is C.

18 Marie Curie, as a single mother, provided education for her daughters by organising lessons for them by specialists in different fields.

The other options are incorrect. The mothers in these texts are not said to take responsibility for the education of any of their children.

19 Ashputtel's mother misleads her daughter and breaks her promise to her.

The other options are incorrect. The mothers in these texts appear trustworthy and honourable.

20 William's mother is strict with her son and makes him do as she thinks he should. However, when he becomes distraught about being late to the fair, she relents and shows her softer side by telling him to take his food with him and not to forget his spending money.

A and B are incorrect. It is not revealed whether Marie Curie or Peggy are less strict than they pretend to be in their roles as mothers.

D is incorrect. Ashputtel's mother is the opposite of this. She is stricter than she pretends to be and is in fact quite cruel.

21 Both Irene and Eva achieved worldwide acclaim for their work that is similar to the acclaim achieved by their mother.

The other options are incorrect. We are not told in these texts of children who follow in their mother's footsteps.

22 The daughter writes in the active voice and uses the personal pronoun 'I' frequently to share personal thoughts and anecdotes. The colloquial language (reckon; let me tell you) adds to the feeling of a speaking voice sharing confidences.

A is incorrect. The tone is formal and distant rather than confiding.

C and D are incorrect. Although both narratives include conversations, the tone

and language of the conversations is not confiding.

23 Tension builds between mother and son as she makes him obey her against his will. As his anxieties about being late for the fair increase, so the tension between them escalates. Her allowing him to take his pudding with him breaks the tension.

A and B are incorrect. The building of tension is not part of the structure of these texts.

D is incorrect. Although tension builds as to whether Ashputtel will get her task done in time or whether she'll realise what her mother is up to, it does not build directly between Ashputtel and her mother. Ashputtel remains overjoyed and rejoices in the possibility she'll be allowed to attend the ball and doesn't realise her mother has been deceiving her all along.

24 Ashputtel represents female innocence and goodness while her mother represents female wickedness and evil in this fairytale.

The other options are incorrect. None of the characters in these texts are stereotypes of good or evil.

25 Peggy's daughter looks up to her mother for dealing with some difficult things in her past and for bravely standing up for her beliefs.

A is incorrect. Although we assume Irene and Eva admire their mother, we are not told in this text what it is they admire about her.

C is incorrect. William is at odds with his mother in this text.

D is incorrect. It is not suggested in this text that Ashputtel admires her mother.

SAMPLE Test 10   Page 68

1 C 2 D 3 D 4 C 5 A 6 B 7 D 8 B 9 C
10 B 11 A 12 F 13 A 14 C 15 D 16 G
17 E 18 B 19 D 20 A 21 B 22 C 23 A
24 C 25 D

1 When Alice realises her shrinking in size means she may now be able to get into the garden, her face brightens. This implies how pleased she feels at this thought.

   A is incorrect. Whether or not she is nervous is not mentioned.

   B and D are incorrect. There is no reference to her disliking being tall or liking the feeling of shrinking.

2 All Alice wants to do is get into the garden she thinks is lovely. When it becomes clear that no matter what she does, she will not be able to enter the garden, she begins to cry.

   A is incorrect. Alice played croquet long ago and she didn't cry but boxed her own ears.

   B and C are incorrect. Not being able to climb up the table leg (B) and forgetting she needs a key to unlock the gate (C) are both part of the frustration that led to her tears. Her tears, though, are mainly caused by her failure to get into the garden.

3 The author uses the word 'curious' to suggest Alice behaves in ways that are different from what is considered normal or expected.

   A is incorrect. Although the writer may think of Alice as special, that is not what he means by the word 'curious' in this context.

   B and C are incorrect. Although the word 'curious' can mean eager to learn or inquisitive, it is not used in that sense here.

4 Alice puts her hand on her head after asking which way because she wants to work out whether the cake has made her smaller or taller.

   A and B are incorrect. She uses the word 'way' to refer to the direction her body is moving of its own accord, not the direction she needs to follow to get to the garden.

   D is incorrect. She thinks her question has been answered: she seems to have stayed the same size so doesn't need to worry about eating the cake.

5 Alice's reaction to finding her feet far away is to concoct highly imaginative and amusing ways of dealing with the situation.

   B is incorrect. There is nothing for the reader to puzzle over or be in doubt about in the way she reacts.

   C is incorrect. Alice reacts by inventing a piece of 'nonsense'; this serves as an aside or pause in the building of tension in the story.

   D is incorrect. Alice's reaction to finding her feet so far away is to think about the consequences in a playful, lighthearted way.

6 Alice reminds herself she is too grown up to cry by referring to herself as 'a great girl like you'. The author adds '(she might well say this)' partly to agree with her but also to slyly hint at another reason. Alice is also 'great' in the sense of enormously tall: she reaches the roof and is more than nine feet high!

   A is incorrect. The author is agreeing with Alice but not necessarily showing approval of her actions.

   C is incorrect. The author doesn't disagree with her; rather he agrees with her in more ways than she realises.

   D is incorrect. It is Alice who points out she is quite grown up—something his comment confirms.

7 The movements of the river cat (a type of ferry) on the water as it moves towards the wharf are compared with those of a cat: it 'creeps', 'sweeps in', 'rubs' and 'scratches' at the wharf as it draws up beside it.

   A is incorrect. The river cat is not literally a cat; it's a ferry.

   B and C are incorrect. Neither the water nor the salt from the water moves like a cat; they don't 'scratch' at the wharf.

8 The 'rusting remnants of industry' refer to leftovers from past industrial activities that have begun to rot or decay.

   A is incorrect. The convicts carried out some of the industry but are not what was left over from it.

C is incorrect. The ghosts who visit the island are spirits and people, not things.

D is incorrect. '[T]he arching bridge' is the bridge in the city that 'others' sail towards; it is not on the Island.

9 It is the giant-like appearance of the cranes that is implied by the phrase 'titan birds'. They stand tall with long noses or beaks, looking like large birds ready to attack their prey.

A is incorrect. They are described as being still, not hopping about.

B is incorrect. They are linked with cockatoos in terms of when they inhabited the island, not in terms of appearance.

D is incorrect. The crane referred to in this context is not a bird; it is a machine.

10 'Voyager, Vampire and an Empress' are said to come into being through industry on the Island. As a dockyard and in its position on Sydney Harbour, and because at least two of the names (Voyager and Empress) are often given to ships, it is very likely these are the names of ships built there.

A is incorrect. They are made on the Island.

C is incorrect. It is not common to give individual names, particularly of this kind, to machines.

D is incorrect. Although ghosts from the past are mentioned, their identities are not individualised or named.

11 The poet imagines the nameless ghosts of the Island's past, those who've lived and worked at Cockatoo Island throughout its varied history, shouting their stories of injustice and suffering to the tourists who visit it.

The other options are incorrect. These are the people who would be haunted by the ghosts' sad stories.

12 In the previous sentence the author gives a definition of a laureate. This sentence explains the origin of the word: It comes from the Latin word *laureatus* meaning 'crowned with a laurel wreath'. The sentence that follows explains what laureates wear to celebrate when they are awarded this honour.

13 In the previous sentence the author states there are many achievements recognised by the award of the title 'laureate'. This sentence gives examples of awards of this type: For example, there are Nobel Laureates and Poet Laureates. The sentence that follows lists countries where Children's Laureates are awarded.

14 In the previous sentence the author tells who introduced the Australian Children's Laureate Award in Australia. This sentence gives information about their logo: Their logo is the Australian magpie. The sentence that follows explains why this particular logo was chosen.

15 In the previous sentence the author names the winners of the award for 2012 to 2013. This sentence gives more information about the first named recipient, Alison Lester: Alison has written over 30 books including well-known titles such as *Ernie Dances to the Didgeridoo* and *Are We There Yet?* The sentence that follows explains what Alison aimed to do when she undertook the role.

16 In the previous sentence the author gives information about Boori Monty Pryor. This sentence gives more information about him: He is a performer: a storyteller, a didgeridoo player, a dancer, a public speaker and filmmaker. The sentence that follows refers to his awards and names some of his books.

17 In the previous sentence the author says that Ursula asked children to act out a story at her laureate ceremony. This sentence tells what the story was about: The story was about ants going on an important expedition with each taking something useful for their journey. The sentence that follows tells what the littlest ant chose to take on their journey.

The unused sentence is B.

18 Both Anne and her teacher express anger for different reasons.

A and C are incorrect. Anger is not expressed.

D is incorrect. Molly's anger is felt but not expressed.

19 Molly's father thinks it best for Molly not to show her feelings when he is sending her away. Molly holds back her feelings until she is alone.

The other options are incorrect. They do not refer to the idea of keeping your feelings repressed.

20 Heidi's eyes are alight with joy because she is with a friend in her favourite spot surrounded by the beauty of nature.

B and D are incorrect. There are no joyful feelings to explain.

C is incorrect. Although feelings of quiet happiness occur, they are not the same as joyfulness.

21 Anne's fury with Gilbert for calling her 'Carrots' turns into physical violence when she smashes her slate on his head.

The other options are incorrect. None of these texts contain any violent actions.

22 Ellie hopes Rebecca asking her to be the first to sign her plaster is a sign of friendship which may lead to them becoming good friends in the future.

A is incorrect. The ending of this text raises a note of sadness.

B is incorrect. This text ends on a note of despair.

D is incorrect. This text ends in Molly's tears.

23 The doctor asks Heidi how to heal a sad heart that he doesn't know how to cure.

B and C are incorrect. These texts are not about sadness.

D is incorrect. Although it is clear Molly is saddened by her father's behaviour and bursts into tears, it is not suggested her tears will make her sadness go away.

24 Jack and Elly are both happy and pleased about things but their feelings are not described as intense.

The other options are incorrect. They all describe intensely felt, passionate feelings: Heidi's joyfulness (A); Anne's furious anger (B); and Molly's unhappiness and despair (D).

25 Molly is distressed because she feels shut out by her father and his 'new wife that was to be'.

A and B are incorrect. These texts are not about feeling excluded.

C is incorrect. Although the quarrel may have had something to do with Rebecca excluding Ellie from being her friend, this is not confirmed.

NOTES

NOTES

NOTES